Love and Life
Parent Guide

Love and Life

A Christian Sexual Morality Guide for Teens

Parent Guide

by Coleen Kelly Mast

Revised Edition

IGNATIUS PRESS   SAN FRANCISCO

Nihil obstat: Very Rev. Joseph J. Tapella
               Vicar General
               Diocese of Joliet, Illinois

Imprimatur: + Most Rev. Joseph L. Imesch,
               Diocese of Joliet
               July 5, 2005

The *nihil obstat* and *imprimatur* are official declarations that a book or pamphlet is free of doctrinal or moral error. No implication is contained therein that those who have granted the *nihil obstat* and *imprimatur* agree with the contents, opinions, or statements expressed in that work.

BananaStock FamilyTeens p. 14, 16, 18, 19, 20, 24, 25, 29, 46, 48, 49, 51, 54, 55, 60, 61; Corbis Modern Teen Vol. 231 p. 12, 32, 52, 53, 59, 64, 65; ImageState Photos by Donna Day p. 11, 43, 45, 57, 58, 62, 63, 65; LifeArt p. 34; PhotoDisc Friends and Family Vol. 121 p. 31, 37, 39, 40; PhotoDisc Life is Good p. 38

Cover photo by Donna Day / ImageState
Design and production by Hespenheide Design
Illustrated by Robert Greisen and Gregory P. Hartnell

Printed in the United States of America

CONTENTS

CHAPTER 5: PARISH IMPLEMENTATION OF *LOVE AND LIFE*

Education in chastity
is about how and when
we hand over the astonishing gift of self.

We choose the setting. We choose the timing.

God gives us the choice.
The lies of the world disguise the true choices.

We can choose to live love to the fullest in all its mystery, or
steal glimpses of its pleasures while corrupting the greatest possibilities of the gift.

We can have it all with God's plan or
we can settle for less with the world's plan:

A love life of grace with the
disappearance of shame
or
a sex life of sin with the accompanying
guilt and shame.

Youth who have squandered their power to love
say they are
disappointed
lonely
sad
feeling a deep sense of loss —
but the loss is hard to describe in words.
Only the healing power of Christ can save.

Human beings desire a love relationship
that will last.
A sure thing.

To be sure,
be pure.

This book is for parents who want to educate their children
about God's plan for human sexuality and help them develop the virtue of chastity.

INTRODUCTION

How can the *Love and Life* program help me as a parent?

Love and Life is a positive, confidence-building program designed to meet the spiritual and educational needs of teenagers or preteens who are maturing physically, emotionally and psychologically into young men and women. The student book focuses on the beauty and harmony of God's plan for love and life. It helps us to recognize and understand that plan and to realize that the practice of the virtue of chastity is integral to a happy, full and successful life.

What is chastity?

The virtue of chastity can be defined as the power to express our human sexuality according to God's plan for creation. Chastity is the virtue that frees romantic love from selfishness and aggressiveness. Chastity includes sexual self-control, and is enriched by grace. The teachings in the *Love and Life* program recognize that our sexuality was created by God and given to us by God. Sexuality, therefore, means more than our individual physical appearance. It is a part of our entire being, and it pervades our thoughts, personalities and relationships for all of our lives. As a gift from God, sexuality expressed through the virtue of chastity can help your teen come to know the fullness of God's love. On the other hand, sexuality can also be used as a way of rejecting God's love. This course helps us to understand the difference between accepting God and rejecting Him. Chastity is part of God's plan for each person. Chastity allows us to be good stewards of God's precious gift of love, in view of giving ourselves back to Him through our vocation to marriage, priesthood or consecrated religious life.

What role do I play as a parent?

The *Love and Life* program encourages you as the parent to be the primary educator of your child, as has always been taught by the Catholic Church. You, as parent, are the one who is in the best position on a daily basis to show your child that the love of God and a life of virtue are the foundation of human happiness. The *Love and Life* program gives you a tool for communicating this message to your teen, whether or not you ever learned it from your own parents. The virtue of chastity gives your teen the ability to enjoy God's gift of life without all the sexual pressures and romantic problems that can hinder emotional, psychological and spiritual growth.

What is the basic message of the text?

God is love. He loves us, created us in His image, and has a beautiful plan for our lives that we are free to live out or reject. God's plan offers true freedom, joy and the holiness that comes through sacrifice.

The use of our sexual gifts as the physical expression of love is discussed in the context of the Sacrament of Marriage. Since marriage is a relatively distant future event for most teens, understanding the role of sexuality outside of marriage is more immediate. *Love and Life* focuses on positive, wholesome attitudes toward personal growth and suggestions for friendships, dating and activities that help teenagers develop into mature, responsible and happy adults.

Why and where should this program be used?

Educating youth and parents about the value of chastity has been strongly encouraged by the

Church. In light of the culture's obsession with sexual pleasure and the widespread misuse of sexuality, education in chastity has become an urgent need for one's soul, happiness and health. *Love and Life* meets this need in a positive and concrete way. The program can be used at home, in school, in parent-teen discussion groups, at retreats or in a parish. It should always involve you, the parent. If someone outside the home administers the student discussions, that person should believe, live and be able to defend the Church's teachings on sexual morality. ***The parents should read the* Student Guide *before their teen, and then accompany their child through the course with this* Parent Guide.**

The value of chastity is seriously challenged by our contemporary society. People are often treated as objects of pleasure. The exploitation of sex in television, film, advertising, Internet and other media trivializes sexual expression as simply a plaything or toy. By equating sex with pleasure and nothing more, the media lose sight of the beauty of our human sexuality as a means of expressing the commitment of lasting love through the sharing of life-giving powers. The culture reduces a sacred form of personal union to a common bodily activity. By presenting the joys and freedom of chastity as more meaningful and appealing than the empty fantasy of "free sex", we can help to prevent the problems created by sexual license and pass on to our youth the fullness of the gift of love and life. Due to the constant bombardment of the negative messages of the culture, parents must be watchful and diligent before and after this course for the sake of their child's future.

Why can't I just let my teen learn from his friends or school?

Parents cannot ignore education for chastity because we are not just talking about sexual information. What is at stake here is the truth of the human person and the meaning and purpose of human sexuality. Also at stake is the human dignity of your child, as well as his future vocation and eternal happiness.

The responsibility to provide our youth with the moral aspects of their human sexuality is clearly stated in the encyclical of Pope John Paul II entitled *Familiaris Consortio* (hereafter FC):

> In view of the close links between the sexual dimension of the person and his or her ethical values, education must bring the children to knowledge of and respect for the moral norms as the necessary and highly valuable guarantee for responsible personal growth in human sexuality.
>
> For this reason the Church is firmly opposed to an often widespread form of imparting sex information dissociated from moral principles. That would merely be an introduction to the experience of pleasure and a stimulus leading to the loss of serenity—while still in the years of innocence—by opening the way to vice. (no. 37)

Moral guidance is a primary responsibility of parents, as stressed in a recent Church document by the Pontifical Council for the Family, *The Truth and Meaning of Human Sexuality* (hereafter TM):

> Parents are rich in an educative potential which no one else possesses. (no. 7)
>
> The Church has always affirmed that parents have the duty and the right to be the first and the principal educators of their children. (no. 5)
>
> In the framework of educating the young person for self-realization and self-giving, formation in chastity implies the collaboration first and foremost of the parents, as is the case with formation for the other virtues such as temperance, fortitude and prudence. (no. 5)

In another Church document, *Educational Guidance in Human Love* (hereafter EG), the Church emphasizes positive and prudent sex education:

> The harmonious development of the human person progressively reveals in each of us the image of a child of God. "True education aims at the formation of the human person with respect to his ultimate goal" (Vatican II, Gravissimum educationis, no. 1). Treating

Introduction

Christian education, Vatican Council II drew attention to the necessity of offering "a positive and prudent sex education" (ibid.) to children and youth. (no. 1)

The teachings of the Church remind us of our true nature, that we are created in the image of God. They urge us toward our ultimate goal, union with God. A positive and prudent sex education helps us reflect on our true nature and helps each of us reach our ultimate goal, eternal ecstasy in Heaven. As parents, we have the responsibility to instill in our children the understanding of our true nature and our purpose in life.

Working through the *Love and Life* program will help you to fulfill your responsibility to your teenagers, while communicating with them in a way that is open, genuine, truthful and rewarding.

> The fecundity of conjugal love cannot be reduced solely to the procreation of children, but must extend to their moral education and their spiritual formation. "The *role of parents in education* is of such importance that it is almost impossible to provide an adequate substitute." (*Gravissimum educationis*, no. 3)—*Catechism of the Catholic Church*, no. 2221

INNOCENT BUT NOT IGNORANT

My parents never talked to me about sex, and I did just fine. Why can't we just do the same?

This question reflects the sentiments many feel when considering their own introduction to human sexuality. Somehow, without any formal instruction or counseling, people have learned the information they needed to know. Or did they? Adults who have received their sex education exclusively from the secular culture have missed out on the true meaning and purpose of human sexuality. They often have difficulty accepting, explaining or defending the teachings of the Church, which they were never taught.

Unfortunately, in the time span of one or two generations, the attitudes of our society toward sex have been altered dramatically. The exploitation of sex for personal gain and pleasure has become all too common, as is evident every day on television, in movies, in popular music, in magazines, in advertising and elsewhere. Here, sex is devoid of even the hint of any purpose other than the gratification of physical urges, and our children are exposed to this on an ongoing basis.

The Church has recognized this danger and tells us the following:

> Silence is not a valid norm of conduct in this matter, above all when one thinks of the "hidden persuaders" which use insinuating language. Their influence today is undeniable: it is up to parents, therefore, to be alert not only to repair the harm caused by inappropriate and injurious interventions, but above all to inform opportunely their own children, offering them a positive and convincing education. (EG, no. 106)

Empower Teens with the Truth

As our children approach adolescence they are preparing to face peers, neighbors and co-workers who are hostile to the teachings of Christ and His Church. One task of adolescent growth is to find one's place in society. This is a frightening thought in a hedonistic and secular world. You parents will need to empower your teen with the information in the *Love and Life: Student Guide* and with considerable doses of the information here in the *Love and Life: Parent Guide*. We want our children to be confident in knowing that they possess the truth about human sexuality.

What a Task in Today's Culture!

Parents today need to repair the harm done to their children by our promiscuous, self-indulgent culture. At the same time they must be positive and convincing in showing that sexuality is sacred and good when expressed according to God's plan. This isn't easy. However, it can be done with God's help. It can be done by teaching our youth about God's plan and motivating them to be Christ-like in their expression of sexuality in accordance with their age, maturity and state in life. It can be done with God's grace, as we continue to pray with and for our children.

With this in mind, let's challenge ourselves to answer the following questions:

- What are our goals for education in human sexuality and chastity?
- What does it mean to educate in a positive and prudent way?
- What benefits does chastity education provide for the family?

What Are Our Goals?

Educating our youth in human sexuality could be done for many reasons, some better than others. Here are several:

1. To get them married before they get pregnant.
2. To make sure they know the correct names of each reproductive organ.
3. To know what is right or wrong in the use of their sexuality.
4. To have wholesome attitudes about sex and its use throughout their lives.
5. To provide them with the freedom to answer God's call for their vocation, whether to marriage, priesthood or consecrated religious life.

If our goal is only avoiding unwed pregnancy, we've only just begun. With merely a superficial mind-set, people might try to justify the use of harmful contraceptives. The trouble with this goal is that fornication, not pregnancy, is a sin. Protecting our teens from the consequences of their actions is not enough. As parents, we have an obligation to do more.

If number two is our goal, we can leave it up to the biology teacher. Since many of us don't remember the clinical names of our anatomy, we may think that a textbook can do a better job than we can. However, the simple study of anatomy does nothing to impart the truth that we are spiritual, as well as physical, beings created in the image and likeness of God. The Church warns us to avoid education in the mechanics of sex that does not include the purpose and meaning of it. Discussing intimate topics at home—where they should be discussed—can help us become closer to our teens during these important years of formation. These family bonds help us stay in touch and guide our teens toward a healthy and holy sexuality.

Goal number three, knowing what is right and wrong, requires that teens have clear direction in conducting their relationships. However, they also need to know why and how to choose God's plan, and need some motivation to do so. It helps to have a higher purpose in mind, such as truly trying to please God, so that we can come to know the joy of His life-giving and life-saving love. Youth need the spiritual guidance of knowing they have God's love and grace to help them. They need the support of their parents to live out the demands of real love.

By going further and helping teens to develop wholesome attitudes toward human sexuality and providing them with the freedom to answer God's call to their particular vocation, we can accomplish all of the aims we have discussed. In other words, by directing our efforts toward the higher goals, we will also satisfy the more basic needs of educating our teens.

The Vatican document *The Truth and Meaning of Human Sexuality* teaches us these higher objectives:

> Educating children for chastity strives to achieve three objectives:
>
> a) to maintain in the family *a positive atmosphere of love, virtue and respect for the gifts of God*, in particular the gift of life;
>
> b) to help children to understand the value of sexuality and chastity in stages, sustaining their growth through enlightening word, example and prayer;
>
> c) to help them understand and discover *their own vocation to marriage or to consecrated virginity for the sake of the Kingdom of Heaven* in harmony with and respecting their attitudes and inclinations and the gifts of the spirit. (no. 22)

The Benefits of Education for Chastity

While educating our teens in the virtue of chastity, we can prepare them to love God and seek His will for a lifetime. Positive steps toward reaching this goal include

1. Helping them develop a personal relationship with God through prayer
2. Teaching our children to understand and master their feelings and desires
3. Challenging them to practice doing good for others, unselfishly
4. Guiding them in developing wholesome friendships
5. Motivating them to save sexual pleasure until it can be experienced in the beauty of the commitment of Christian marriage

Chastity enables our children to have the freedom to embrace their vocation in life without the confusion, hurt and enslavement to sin that result if they behave in a self-centered way and participate in sexual activity outside of marriage.

Chastity enables our children to enjoy the gift of their sexuality within marriage, if that is their vocation, in a way that brings Christ into their marriage and reflects His unselfish love. If their call is to priesthood or consecrated religious life, it is just as important to have an understanding of the meaning and purpose of human sexuality. Also necessary is the virtue of chastity, for through the practice of chastity, they will come to appreciate their power to love and be loved in a fully human, though not sexually arousing, way. They will be free to focus all their love on God and His people.

What Does a Positive and Prudent Education in Sexuality Really Mean?

> In a positive and prudent way parents will carry out what the Fathers of the Second Vatican Council requested: "It is important to give suitable and timely instruction to young people, above all in the heart of their own families, about the dignity of married love, its role and its exercise; in this way they will be able to engage in honorable courtship and enter upon marriage of their own." (TM, no. 94)

The words *positive* and *prudent* occur frequently in Church documents when describing sex education. Let's examine what they mean.

Positive education affirms goodness and truth. God is Truth. His plan is truth. Our youth today are hungry for truth. In an age of incessant exaggeration and distortion in advertising, it is refreshing to hear the truth. Developing the virtue of chastity frees us and enables us to develop the other skills needed in relationships and in successful marriages, such as the art of verbal communication. Our approach to moral teaching must be positive and affirmative, not merely defensive or apologetic. We need to show our teens the beauty of virtue and the joy of living as a Christian.

Prudent means "with good judgment". We need to use care and discretion in sharing sexual information with our children. As a gift of God, our sexuality must be respected and cherished as the beautiful gift that it is. Slang expressions and the language of the street are inappropriate. If we want our children to respect their sexuality, we must speak of it with respect ourselves. It is our own good judgment in language, dress and behavior that shows them that we are happiest when we accept and reflect God's love for us.

Don't Overwhelm Them with Sexual Information

Prudence suggests that we not overwhelm our youth with too much biological information. Most of us have heard the story of the young mother who was asked by her six-year-old son, "Where did I come from?" The mother, who considered herself to be well prepared, had been waiting for the subject to come up and proceeded to explain fertility, conception and pregnancy. Her son, somewhat bored, interrupted her with, "Mom, the new boy in our class came from Philadelphia. Where did I come from?"

Most young teens have a keen sense of modesty and innocence. We want to build on that, not desensitize it. Movies, television programs and songs on the radio often present sex as a sport or game. This irreverent treatment can be confusing, misleading and even harmful to the attitudes of a young Christian. Media images can remain in our imaginations until we begin to think that deviant sexuality is in some way normal. It is important to limit our

own and our child's exposure to such distortions, so that we can help him foster attitudes of respect and reverence reflective of Christian principles.

Prudence is required in order to protect a child's innocence. The tender years preceding puberty are described in Church teachings on sexuality as an "age of innocence" that must be protected. Psychologists often call this the *latency period*, and the Church urges us to respect and protect this time by not burdening children with unnecessary sexual information. For example, innocent preteens do not need descriptions of deviant sexual acts. They might know that such behaviors occur, but they don't need to know more. A young and innocent teen may not even require a description of sexual intercourse until he needs it or specifically asks for it. Simple phrases such as "the marital union" or "becoming one flesh" can be enough. Stay in close communication with your teen, however, so you will be aware of his level of exposure to sources of information outside the family.

Answer Questions Honestly, Simply

When questions are asked about delicate issues, our answers should be honest, simple and respectful of the child's age. If we don't know the answer, we need to say so and offer to find it. Hopefully, the teachings in this *Parent Guide* will help you through many of those questions.

Sometimes the questions asked by a teenager may seem like attacks on morals, but usually they are not. Most of the time they are attempts to understand. We need to help our teens to feel comfortable talking with us. If we don't help them to understand their sexuality in the light of Christ, they will seek understanding elsewhere.

If we fill their minds and hearts first with the goodness and truth of chaste love, teens can better judge sexual immorality for what it is—false and disordered. Their solid knowledge can help them look past the trash magazine stand or the newspaper ads and reject the shallow, hedonistic views they represent.

Be Attentive to Their World of Influences

It is important to know what's going on with your children and their friends. There is a balance between violating innocence and pretending that our teens never think about or hear about sex. Staying in touch through daily listening will help you know

Atmosphere in the Home for Teaching Chastity

1. The atmosphere in the home should be harmonious, with husband and wife valuing a peaceful relationship.

2. On an ongoing basis, instruct the children in charity (generous love), temperance (moderation and self-control) and fortitude (courage to do what is right).

3. Parents should find time to be with their children and take time to talk with them.

4. Teach children how to develop positive relationships with God, brothers, sisters and companions.

5. Teach self-control and self-restraint in all areas of life, demonstrating how to live in an orderly way, and how to make sacrifices in the spirit of love for God, respecting oneself while being generous toward others.

6. Discipline your children. An undisciplined or spoiled child is inclined toward a certain immaturity and moral weakness in future years, making chastity difficult.

7. Parents must actively ensure a moderate, critical, watchful and prudent use of the media.

8. The greatest example of love that parents can give is to be generous in accepting new lives into the family, building a community of love. This calls for sacrifice, helps naturally fight individualism and selfishness and enables a large family to more easily reject consumerism and materialism by adopting a simpler lifestyle.

9. In order to achieve these objectives, the family should first be a home of faith and prayer in which God's presence is sensed, the word of Jesus is accepted, the Spirit's bond of love is felt and where the most pure Mother of God is loved and invoked.

10. Parents have a duty to let their children know about the mysteries of human life because the home is the best environment for this gradual and individualized education at the appropriate times.

11. In talks with your children, suitable advice should always be given regarding how to grow in the love of God and one's neighbor and how to overcome difficulties. The means to do these are: the discipline of the senses and the mind; watchfulness and prudence in avoiding occasions of sin; the observance of modesty, moderation in recreation, wholesome pursuits, assiduous prayer, and frequent reception of the sacraments of Penance and Eucharist.

(Adapted from *The Truth and Meaning of Human Sexuality*, Pontifical Council for the Family, 1995.)

your teen. Get to know your teen's friends, activities and attitudes. A shy and innocent girl who associates with more aggressive, boy-crazy friends may need to discuss questions and feelings about herself, those she sees, and what is going on around her. It's never too early to talk about dressing modestly and adopting Christ-like attitudes toward people of the opposite sex.

A junior-high boy who has not yet known his first wet dream or sexual attraction may still need to discuss his own growth, the temptations he may face, even in his dreams, and how to practice self-control.

> Parents should be close to their sons and correct the tendency to use sexuality in a hedonistic and materialistic way. Therefore, they should remind boys about God's gift, received in order to cooperate with Him . . . The parent's task of informing and instructing is necessary, not because their sons would not know about sexual reality in other ways, but so that they will know about it in the right light. (TM, no. 93)

Parents must be extra attentive if their teens are exposed to sexual misinformation through friends, school and the secular media. The world of advertisers and wild talk shows has an answer to every one of your teen's questions—but usually an answer that will not lead your child to goodness and virtue. Be aware of what your child is hearing and seeing. Help him avoid all the bad influences you can, and teach him to think through the information he already has been exposed to with such questions as: How does this conform to God's plan? How does it diverge from God's plan? Are people who do or say those things respectful? Truly happy? Really loving? Respectful of life? Respectful of the human person made in the image and likeness of God? Thinking of the spiritual and physical consequences? Are they seeking instant pleasure or gratification at the cost of long-term love and fulfillment?

Radiate Human Dignity and Joy

Finally, prudent sex education is careful not to degrade sex. To make fun of others and their sexuality, to tell off-color jokes or to offer contraceptives to a child will send the wrong message. Sex is not dirty, nor is it a joke. Sex is not an urge simply to be indulged. Our human sexuality should be treated respectfully as a human, holy, powerful and marvelous gift.

One teen described the gift of procreation with these awe-filled words: "Just think about it. God has asked us as mere humans to join Him—God—in co-creating a new being and sharing His love! And all He asks is that we wait until marriage."

> The objective of the parent's educational task is to pass on to their children the conviction that chastity in one's state of life is possible and that chastity brings joy. Joy springs from an awareness of maturation and harmony in one's emotional life, a gift of God and a gift of love that makes self-giving possible in the framework of one's vocation. Man is in fact the only creature on earth whom God wanted for his own sake, and "man can fully discover his true self only in a sincere giving of himself." (TM, no. 73)

Discipline and Self-Control

In addition to giving specific instruction on human sexuality education, *The Truth and Meaning of Human Sexuality* reminds us how to prepare our children for chastity well before puberty, by disciplining them and teaching them self-control.

> As in the first years of life also during childhood, parents should encourage a spirit of collaboration, obedience, generosity and self-denial in their children, as well as a capacity for self-reflection and sublimation. . . .

> An undisciplined or spoiled child is inclined toward a certain immaturity and moral weakness in future years because chastity is difficult to maintain if a person develops selfish or disordered habits and cannot behave with proper concern and respect for others. Parents should present objective standards of what is right and wrong, thereby creating a sure moral framework for life. (no. 86)

Benefits for the Family

Virtue in the Home

When our goal is holiness, our children can see chastity as one of the many virtues we practice. As we challenge our children to live virtuous lives, we hear God call us to be good examples ourselves. When our children witness our marital fidelity and the power and blessings of the Sacrament of Matrimony brought about by following the teachings of the Church on marriage, they will want these same benefits for their own marriages. Our example must be an open and honest witness.

No family is perfect, however, and our holy witness includes our struggles in life. We admit our mistakes and learn from them, seek forgiveness and act toward one another with compassion and understanding.

The power to witness the love of God within family life is offered through the graces of the Sacrament of Matrimony, and strengthened by the Sacraments of Penance and Eucharist. Our cultural conditioning has taken us so far from God that we must draw upon the sacraments as frequently as possible to remain close to Him.

Family Bonds

Talking about intimate subjects such as God, sex and chastity can help develop closeness and trust between our children and us. There is no better place for this discussion than at home. A 2002 study in the *Journal of Adolescent Health* reported that a close personal connection between parent and child is an invisible force that protects teens from the peer pressure to have sex outside of marriage

If sexuality is a forbidden subject at home, we can be creating barriers between us and our children, or unspoken attitudes that suggest everything about sex is dirty. Sex is holy and good within God's plan, and parents are the best teachers of this truth. Experiencing and discussing God's plan for love and life creates a wonderful bond for the family.

> The fact remains ever valid that with regard to the more intimate aspects, whether biological or affective, an individual education should be bestowed, preferably within the sphere of the family. (EG, no. 58)

> The family environment is thus the normal and usual place of forming children and young people to consolidate and exercise the virtues of charity, temperance, fortitude and chastity. As the domestic church, the family is the school of the richest humanity. (TM, no. 48)

An Example to the World

"You are the light of the world. . . . Let your light so shine before men, that they may see your good works and give glory to your Father who is in heaven" (Matthew 5:14–16). All of our Catholic Christian families are called to reflect the love of Christ, to be a little church—a beacon of light to the world.

Many other parents are struggling with teaching chastity and other virtues in their homes. What better teacher is there for our neighbors and acquaintances than a good example of a well-formed family? Although the state of immorality in our media and culture is not going to change overnight, we must begin somewhere and with someone— ourselves. On an individual basis, we can create a respect for sexuality in the next generation by forming our children in the truth. They will be the ones to eliminate the demand for abortion, pornography and contraceptives. Dream big! We can begin to renew the world, one family at a time. "It only takes a spark to get a fire going!"

Parents—Growing in Confidence to Represent Christ

As parents, we already have the common sense that comes with age and experience. We also have the

grace of state that God gives us to carry out our duty as Christian parents. Sure, teens will say that times have changed. However, human nature has not changed, God has not changed, and eternal truth means truth that does not change. God's plan is right and true throughout the ages, and it is something that we can believe and teach with confidence.

> The Pontifical Council for the Family therefore urges parents to have confidence in their rights and duties regarding the education of their children, so as to go forward with wisdom and knowledge, knowing that they are sustained by God's gift. In this noble task, may parents always place their trust in God through prayer to the Holy Spirit, the gentle Paraclete and Giver of all good gifts. (TM, no. 150)

Confidence through Prayer

We must never underestimate the power of God. He can touch people in a way that no human word can.

Let us pray for our children before, during and after their teen years. Pray for the individuals they date. Pray for their future spouses. A good idea is to say a family Rosary on Friday evenings for the increase in the virtue of chastity in our society and in ourselves. Let us pray, with our teens, that those involved in sinful use of sex may turn to God for love instead of to an immature dependence on sensuality. Let us pray that our teens will have the strength to resist the temptations they face, and pray that they will develop wholesome sexual attitudes. It is never too late to start praying with our youth. All we need is the determination to begin, and the persistence to keep it up, knowing that we are partners with God, who will give us the confidence we need. God is with us. Let us join our families to Him!

Confidence through the Sacrament of Penance

Children need good role models. However, even if we have made some mistakes ourselves, we need not forfeit our role here. Our calling as parents is to set forth Christian ideals for our children, to serve as examples to the best of our ability and to challenge our children to strive to reach those ideals in their own lives.

Even when we fail, acknowledgment of our failure to God and our determination not to repeat it can serve as an example in itself:

- Maybe you're divorced, but you believe in the commitment of marriage.
- Maybe you had sex before marriage, but you want to spare your own children the negative consequences of that experience.
- Maybe you've used artificial birth control because you didn't accept the Church's teachings or understand the reasoning behind them.
- Maybe you've already suffered from the harmful effects of pornography or other immoral practices.

Even if we've failed on the path of God's design, through the Sacrament of Penance we can gain forgiveness and the confidence we need to guide our children well. We need not teach them to repeat our errors.

Confession is agreeing with God. It's saying, "God, I was wrong, You were right. I'm sorry; please, forgive me, and I'll make every effort not to sin again."

Unfortunately, with some elements of psychology focusing people on the self-justifying concept of "self-esteem", there is a tendency to avoid admitting our failures. Instead of admitting sin and asking for forgiveness, some try to justify their actions with excuses, arguing that sinful behavior is all right under certain circumstances. They try to convince themselves that sexual sins don't really offend God or hurt anyone. This is self-deception.

It is a healthy sign of humility to be able to say, "I'm sorry I offended you, and I'll make every effort not to hurt you again."

How would your relationship be with a person who continually hurt you, but never apologized? Suppose this person always rationalized his behavior?

A barrier would develop between the two of you, and continued friendship would become impossible.

Do you want to work with God in teaching your children virtue? We need to ask for His forgiveness so we don't have a burden of sin to pass on to our children. By getting as close to God as we can, we forge a friendship with the almighty Creator of love and life. Grow in that confidence God offers through the Sacrament of Penance.

Confidence through God's Grace

We have been baptized in Christ and have been confirmed in His Spirit. Christians are supposed to rise above cultural norms that oppose Christ and His Church. Even if the rest of the world has chosen to reject sexual morality, we do not have to follow. We have God's grace and strength.

We have the grace offered to us each day through the Sacrament of the Holy Eucharist. There are adversaries—namely, the world and its material values, a culture that places pleasure and convenience above all else, our own disordered desires and lack of will and even the devil himself. However, God, our All-Powerful Father, has promised us the strength and assistance we need.

With the power of God, we have all the confidence we need. He has conquered sin and death through His own death and resurrection. All we need do is ask Him to send the grace He offers, put on the armor of Christ to grow in virtue, and trust in Him to provide all the strength we need.

Jesus tells us in the Sermon on the Mount:

> Enter by the narrow gate; for the gate is wide and the way is easy, that leads to destruction, and those who enter by it are many. For the gate is narrow and the way is hard, that leads to life, and those who find it are few. (Matthew 7:13–14)

Confidence by Understanding and Integrating the Teachings of the Church

The Catholic Church, as the universal Church, is large and diverse. Through the centuries, it has gained the collective wisdom of countless faithful individuals. The teachings of Jesus Christ are true for every culture and every age. By looking to the teachings of the Church, as given to us by the Holy Spirit, we gain the confidence of knowing that we are on solid ground.

Over time, there have been many ideas on sex education. Some have taken a puritanical approach, which basically states, "Don't talk to the children about sex; it'll give them ideas." This thinking suggests that sex is bad. On the other hand, we have those who proclaim that every sexual act is acceptable, as long as one is trying to be a good person and doesn't hurt anyone. These proponents deny that God has a plan for our sexuality and confuse situation ethics with true morality. Our teens need to develop the virtue of chastity, as the *Love and Life: Student Guide* teaches them, and for this they need knowledge and understanding of themselves and of Church teaching. Such a foundation will strengthen our teens and their future families.

The Vatican document *Educational Guidance in Human Love* tells us:

> In order for the value of sexuality to reach its full realization, *"education for chastity* is absolutely essential, for it is a virtue that develops a person's authentic maturity *and* makes him capable of respecting and fostering the 'nuptial meaning' of the body" (FC, no. 37). It consists in self-control, in the capacity of guiding the sexual instinct to the service of love and of integrating it in the development of the person. Fruit of the grace of God and of our cooperation, chastity tends to harmonize the different components of the human person, and to overcome the frailty of human nature, marked by sin, so that each person can follow the vocation to which God has called him. (no. 18)

The clarity and soundness of our Church teachings on chastity are apparent in her recent declarations. Take the time to read the wisdom and truth in the following Vatican documents, all of which are available online.

> *The Truth and Meaning of Human Sexuality*
> *Educational Guidance in Human Love*
> *Familiaris Consortio [The Christian Family in the*
>   *Modern World]*
> *Vatican Declaration on Sexual Ethics*
> *Humanae Vitae [On Human Life]*
> *Donum Vitae [The Gift of Life]*
> *Evangelium Vitae [The Gospel of Life]*

Our God is a loving God. He has established His Church and in her a love and an authority that continue to proclaim His Word in modern times. He wants us to be happy, and for this reason He wants us to grow to be holy. His teachings tell us, "Here's the best way to grow, and here's the road to true eternal happiness."

Do we answer, "Sorry, God, no thanks. I'll make up my own rules"? Or can we handle the challenge? God knows what's best for us. He created us. He knows us and loves us so much that He continues to give us His word. He knows our weaknesses and promises to be our strength.

To learn more about the depth of Christian love and to gain the confidence to pass on the truth about love to our children, we simply need to learn and integrate the teaching of the Catholic Church.

Confidence Gained in Relationships with Others

- When was the last time I read a book that would help me understand my spouse better?
- When was the last time I really *listened* to a family member in order to understand him better?
- How long has it been since I challenged myself to change, to grow, to know myself more deeply or to be a better person?
- How often do my spouse and I spend time enriching our marriage?
- Do I see my spouse and children as gifts of God?
- Do I pray daily that I will grow to love my spouse and children more deeply?

When we grow in an understanding of ourselves and our family relationships, we gain the confidence to transfer the benefit of this understanding to our children. When we make no attempt to alleviate bitterness, confusion or misunderstanding in our relationships with others, what can we pass on? If our own marital relationship is in continuous discord, what does that say to our children about sex and marriage? For your sake and the sake of your children, please continue to work toward the personal unity in your marriage that God desires for you in order to be good witnesses of God's love.

UNIT BY UNIT— LOVE AND LIFE

Sex education, which is a basic right and duty of parents, must always be carried out under their attentive guidance, whether at home or in educational centers chosen and controlled by them. (FC, no. 37)

Themes and Concepts

In order to give proper attentive guidance throughout the *Love and Life* program, it is necessary to be familiar with the student text. **Please read your child's text in its entirety.** Your child's text is divided into four units, and each unit into several chapters. Here is a summary of the *Love and Life Student Guide*:

- **UNIT ONE—A PLAN FOR OUR HAPPINESS**   Provides an opportunity for parent and teen to develop critical thinking skills in evaluating the culture with the truths of God.
  - **Chapter One—What's It All About?** Defines chastity and emphasizes the value of this virtue in a teen's life today. It includes the sixth and ninth commandments and basic teachings on the family.
  - **Chapter Two—Putting Things in Order** Shows that God is the proper center of all love and life and that exploitation results when sex is made the center of man's life.
  - **Chapter Three—The Great Break-Up** Describes the fall of mankind from a perfect state to an imperfect condition in which our desires for pleasure often conflict with what is best for us. A critical thinking exercise helps teens evaluate secular music in the light of Christ.
  - **Chapter Four—The Great Make-Up** Shows the love of God in giving us Jesus Christ who restored the relationship we have with our Heavenly Father. Reminds us of our call to a life of real love.
  - **Chapter Five—The Real Source and the Real Force** Explains the role of the Church as Christ's Mystical Body, which provides us with grace through the sacraments and guides us with her teachings.

- **UNIT TWO—THE BUILDING BLOCKS OF LOVE AND LIFE**   Offers interesting teachings and exercises for parent and teen to examine life more deeply and to live life more fully.
  - **Chapter Six—Male and Female, He Created Them**   Reveals the goodness of our human sexuality as God created us, male and female, in His image. Includes discussion of sex differentiation and complementarity.
  - **Chapter Seven—A Life of Virtue** Emphasizes that God has created each of us in His own image. By acknowledging our strengths and weaknesses, we can work to fulfill our responsibility to become the best we can be.
  - **Chapter Eight—A Life of Love** Through personal quizzes, we can examine our progress on the road to becoming a great Christian lover of God, our family and our friends.
  - **Chapter Nine—A Life of Friendship** Describes the qualities of true friendship and shows teens how to channel the youthful quest for fun into constructive outlets.

—**Chapter Ten—A Life of Emotional Maturity** Deals with our emotions as indicators of pleasure or pain, not directions for our moral actions. Preparing for feelings of romantic attachment and sexual attraction.

—**Chapter Eleven—Put Yourself in the Driver's Seat—with Self-Mastery** Explains how we have control over our bodily desires, and that we are not slaves to our biological drives.

• **UNIT THREE—THE GREAT RACE** Presents parent and teen discussion topics that develop and articulate norms and boundaries to support the virtue of chastity.

—**Chapter Twelve—The Starting Line** Defines sin as a refusal to obey God, recognizes the importance of forming one's conscience according to God's Law.

—**Chapter Thirteen—Hurdles on the Track to Holiness** Explains that temptation is not a sin until we stop resisting it.

—**Chapter Fourteen—Modesty: a Good "Put-On"** Describes how to develop modesty by having a pure mind, clean speech, proper dress and virtuous actions.

—**Chapter Fifteen—The Chastity Generation** Describes wholesome dating practices, distinguishes love from infatuation and explains how to socialize without jeopardizing purity.

—**Chapter Sixteen—Nature Never Forgives** Distinguishes between the positive results of the practice of chastity and the natural negative consequences of sins against chastity.

—**Chapter Seventeen—Close Encounters of the Best Kind** Points out how the Sacrament of Penance can help us to overcome the spiritual consequences of sin and how this sacrament, as well as the Eucharist, can strengthen us to avoid sin in the future.

—**Chapter Eighteen—The Saints Come Marching In** Provides reminders that there are many chaste people alive today and many saints throughout history who have chosen chastity.

• **UNIT FOUR—THE CALL TO SERVE CHRIST IN LOVE** Opens to the parent and teen the vision of living out their sexuality in accordance with God's will for them.

—**Chapter Nineteen—Let Me Get That Call** Describes how chastity leaves us free to answer God's call to marriage, priesthood or consecrated religious life.

—**Chapter Twenty—To Love and Honor . . . Till Death** Shows the Sacrament of Matrimony as a lifelong commitment to love, based on the beauty and dignity of our Church teachings.

—**Chapter Twenty-One—Love and Life: The Heavenly Bond** To give love and life is the purpose of sexual union. Natural Family Planning enables us to cooperate with the way God made our bodies. Artificial reproductive techniques violate the dignity of human love and life.

—**Chapter Twenty-Two—God Is Pro-Life and Pro-Love** Shows God, and not man, as the Creator, Judge and Sole Proprietor of life, and challenges teens to be in the forefront of the struggle to prevent abortion.

—**Chapter Twenty-Three—Do It for God; He's Done It For You** Reviews the challenge to live this life of love to which we are called.

—**Chapter Twenty-Four—Take the Pledge for Purity** Summarizes the call to chastity and provides an opportunity to take a pledge for purity.

Topics for Home Discussion

The following are suggested questions to discuss as you go through the *Student Guide* with your teen. You may wish to revisit some of the discussion topics as the teen years progress.

Unit One—A Plan for Our Happiness

1. To become mature adults, we must learn to use our sexuality according to God's truth and design. Discuss God's plan for the expression of our human sexuality for love and life.

2. Discuss the meaning of the sixth and ninth commandments. How do the sixth and ninth commandments guide and protect us?

3. Discuss why it is so important to our emotional, physical and spiritual maturity to see our body as a gift from God that must be appreciated and respected.

4. What is original sin? Discuss the effect it has on us as individuals, as families, and as a society.

5. Discuss why it is so important to meditate on and to appreciate Our Lord's life, death and resurrection. What does this paschal mystery say to us about the purpose of suffering in our life? Remembering what St. Paul said about love in his letter to the Corinthians, and how Christ was the perfect lover, what must we do to "walk across the bridge" Jesus rebuilt between Heaven and earth?

6. Using the chart from Chapter 5 of the *Student Guide*, discuss and compare how each of the seven sacraments aids us in developing our spiritual life. Note how the sacraments fulfill spiritual needs that correspond to our physical needs.

7. What are some of the consequences society is paying today as the result of uncontrolled and immature use of sex?

Unit Two—The Building Blocks of Love and Life

1. Discuss the order of the events given by God in Genesis, "Therefore a man leaves his father and his mother and cleaves to his wife, and they become one flesh" (Genesis 2:24).

2. Chapter 7 of the *Student Guide* reviews the virtues needed to grow in confidence and maturity. Discuss why these virtues are so important to our maturing as Christian men and women.

3. Help your teen through the virtue chart in Chapter 7. Approach it with delicacy and prayer —not to ridicule or condemn, but to help improve self-awareness. Promise to make an effort to help one another overcome weaknesses and strengthen virtues. Select one virtue to work on each week, and repeat as needed.

4. Discuss the results of the love quizzes in Chapter 8, and formulate a plan for helping one another grow in love.

5. Why is it important for teens to plan their activities with friends ahead of time? Discuss an example of an activity for two or three friends that is both constructive and fun.

6. Discuss with your teen some of the "crushes" or romances you may have had during high school. Talk about the outcomes if you would like to. Discuss the difference between romantic feelings and real love.

7. Why did God create bodily desires, and when are they good? How can they be a problem? What is the difference between needs and wants?

8. Why did Christ leave us Himself in the Holy Eucharist?

9. How can we make the Holy Mass more fruitful for ourselves?

Unit Three—The Great Race

1. Discuss how enslavement to our bodily desires causes us to lose our freedom to choose.

2. How do the Ten Commandments inform our conscience?

3. There are seven capital sins: pride, envy, greed, lust, anger, sloth (laziness), and gluttony. Discuss how two of these, lust and gluttony, impair our ability to love.

4. How does admitting our sins and taking responsibility for them help us grow and mature?

5. What does the virtue of modesty include? (Hint: a pure mind, clean speech, modest dress and virtuous actions.) Using a magazine or catalog, discuss with your teen clothing that is modest and immodest.

6. Why must we be careful about what we listen to, what we read and what we watch in order to protect our purity?

7. What are your views on dating and courtship? What is the purpose of dating? Why is it better to wait until the early adult years to date? Why is it good to date without kissing?

8. Ask your teen to list the qualities one should look for in a person to date and the qualities one should avoid.

9. "Set your standards of dating conduct before you date so you don't go with the flow of emotion." Why is this important? Set some family rules for dating if you haven't already.

10. Discuss the statement: God always forgives, man sometimes forgives, nature never forgives.

11. Discuss how each of the three steps in the Sacrament of Penance helps to remove guilt.

12. Many saints provide examples of purity. Pick one of the saints and discuss how his or her example can guide you on your path to Heaven.

Unit Four—The Call to Serve Christ in Love

1. Discuss how the graces of the Sacrament of Matrimony help a husband and wife.

2. How does the knowledge that human life begins at conception help us realize that abortion is seriously wrong?

3. The student workbook lists three steps that help us grow in God's love. Explain why they are necessary.

4. What is temperance, and why is it important to living a chaste and holy life?

5. Why should young Catholics develop a devotion to Mary and the Holy Rosary?

6. Discuss the four qualities of married love— human, total, faithful/exclusive, fruitful.

7. Talk about the need for religious vocations. Discuss the possibility of a call to the priesthood or consecrated religious life. What means can teens use to become more open to hearing God's call as to their vocation in life?

Family Activities

These activities coincide with the units in your child's text and will help to reinforce the livable, loveable and good Catholic teachings in *Love and Life*. Plan to do as many as you can with your teen and with the rest of your family. Do it for fun. Do it for love.

Unit I—Getting It Together

1. **Celebrate the sacraments.** Spend an evening remembering the sacraments in your lives. Get out your wedding pictures and photos or mementos of Baptisms, First Communions, First Reconciliations and Confirmations. Recall the excitement, what clothes you wore, your feelings before, during and afterward. Discuss how God has strengthened your family through the sacraments. Have each person share how Sunday Mass helps your family become closer.

2. **Have a respect life night at home.** Get some pictures of life before birth from a book, encyclopedia, pro-life brochure or website. View and discuss the beauty and awe of God's creation and miraculous plan for human growth and development. The computer CD *Life Begins* is available from www.loveandlife.com.

3. **Critique a movie together.** Discuss a movie or television show that you have watched together. How was the meaning of love portrayed? What image of marriage or sex was portrayed? Was there any exploitation of sex or sensuality? Were morals promoted or ignored?

   How did the show present characters suffering the consequences of immoral actions (lying, cheating, fornication)? Was the message simply "No big deal" or "Don't get caught"?

   Could the plot of the show have survived without the immorality? How would you rewrite the plot to illustrate or reinforce Christian morals?

Discuss the commercials. Think of other ways there are to sell products (toothpaste, chewing gum, soft drinks) without relying on sex appeal.

Unit II—God's Gifts

1. **Animals and Humans.** Find a book, movie or educational television show about animal life. Read or watch it together as a family. Discuss what human beings have in common with animals and what unique attributes God has given to us alone.

2. **Acting out emotions.** Review the concepts of emotional maturity in Chapter 10. Have each family member act out some of the different emotions. Discuss the good and bad ways to express emotions at different ages. Help one another think of ways to practice more emotional maturity at home.

Unit III—The Great Race

1. **Attend a weekday Mass as a family.** Find in the Sunday missal or church missalette the next weekday feast of a virgin saint. Plan to attend Mass as a family on this day for the development of virtue in your family. If this means extra sacrifices (getting up early, missing a meal or adjusting a work schedule), this will help emphasize the importance your family places on prayer and virtue over daily conveniences.

2. **Know-your-commandments awareness day.** Select a weekend day when most family members are home. Begin the morning with prayer, and then have someone read and post the Ten Commandments. Discuss the meaning of each one, and have each family member keep track of the temptations against each commandment he experiences throughout the day. At the end of the day, discuss each commandment and how each family member can best observe it.

3. **Forgiveness.** Practice seeking forgiveness within your family at times when you have offended one another. A simple "Will you forgive me?" and the opportunity to say, "Yes, I forgive you," can bring closeness to the forgiver

and the forgiven. Have the whole family attend confession or a penance service this week at your church. If you are not in the habit of making a regular confession already, this is a good time to begin. There is no better example for children than to see their parents participating in the sacraments and challenging themselves to grow more perfect in God's grace.

Unit IV—The Call to Serve Christ in Love

1. **Pray the Rosary as a family.** Three evenings this week, pray the Rosary as a family, reflecting on the Joyful, the Luminous, the Sorrowful or the Glorious Mysteries.
2. **The real meaning of words.** Discuss what it means to be the "salt of the earth" and the "light of the world".
3. **Family fun night.** Plan a unique family fun night using some of the suggested activities in Chapter 9. Try something as a family that you have never done before.

Parent-Teen Questionnaires

The following questionnaires can provide a fun and interesting way to get to know what is on your teen's mind. There is one questionnaire for the parents that corresponds with each of the unit questionnaires in the student book. Fill them out, and then share with your teen answers to the questions you think will be most interesting or helpful.

Unit I Questions for Parents

1. How much time do you normally spend with your teen in a week?
   0–2 hrs.　　2–4 hrs.　　4–6 hrs.
   6–8 hrs.　　8 hrs. or more
2. How often does your teen talk to you about things that are bothering him?
   never　　seldom　　often　　always
3. Can you talk openly and freely with your teen?

   _____

4. Does your family have meals together? If so, is the atmosphere
   relaxed　　tense　　rushed　　pleasant

5. Do you share your faith and your efforts to deepen it with your teen? _____
6. What has your teen done for you that you appreciate? _____
   What have you done for your teen that you hope he appreciates? _____
7. Do you think your teen has enough responsibilities for his age?_____ How is he doing fulfilling them? _____
   Do you think he needs more or less responsibilities? _____
8. Do you know what your teen thinks about fornication (premarital sex)? _____
9. What topics would you like to discuss with your teen? _____
10. How can you and your teen improve your relationship? _____

Unit 2 Parent-Teen Questionnaire: How Well Do You Know Your Adolescent?

1. What makes your teen the happiest?

   _____

   _____

2. What is his greatest sorrow or aggravation?

   _____

   _____

3. Choose the words that best describe your teen.
   happy　　　　　　　moody
   helpful　　　　　　self-absorbed
   busy　　　　　　　idle
4. What is causing your son or daughter the greatest concern right now?
   grades or school　　　friends
   appearance　　　　　physical changes
   family problems　　　other_____
5. What emotional changes have you noticed in your teen that are indicators of adolescence?
   fluctuating dependence and independence
   moodiness　　　　attraction to the opposite sex
   aggressiveness　　need for security
   other _____,
6. What can you and your teen do to help each other learn more about love and life?

   _____

7. Which topics in the emotional maturity chapter would be most helpful for you and your teen to discuss?_____

8. Which topics in the friendship chapter would be most helpful for you and your teen to discuss?

_____

Unit 3 Parent-Teen Questionnaire

If you have not already done so, discuss with your teen the section of this guide called "Is Your Teen Ready to Date?" on pages 57–59, and "How Do You Know If You Are Ready to Date?" in the student workbook on pages 89–90.

Let's Discuss Dating

1. What is the purpose of dating? _____

_____

_____

2. What is a good age to begin:
   group dating_____
   double dating _____
   single dating _____
   steady dating _____
   marriage _____

3. Should there be a dating curfew (limit on time to come in)? What is reasonable?

_____

_____

4. Should you drink on a date (beer, wine, other alcohol)? Why or why not? _____

_____

5. Honest affection should express the depth of your relationship, and not be based only on feelings. What kind of relationship is expressed in each of these forms of affection?
   arms around each other _____
   holding hands _____
   goodnight kiss _____
   hugging or cuddling _____

Questions for Further Discussion

What is the difference between love and infatuation?
How do you ask a girl on a date?
How do you say no without hurting feelings?
What do you do on a date?
If your date does something you don't agree with, what should you do?
How do you say no to sexual advances?
What should one look for in a marriage partner?

Unit 4 Parent-Teen Questionnaire

1. What are we doing in our family to encourage religious vocations? _____

_____

2. Do we express any attitudes that discourage religious vocations? _____

_____

3. What advantages are there to a chaste single life? _____

_____

4. What can we do in our family that will allow our teens the freedom to hear their calling in life? _____

_____

5. What should a person look for in a future marriage partner? _____

_____

6. Why are sacramental graces needed for marriage? _____

_____

7. What is Natural Family Planning? How is it different from artificial birth control? _____

_____

_____

8. Name some serious reasons for spacing or limiting the number of children in marriage?_____

_____

9. What attitudes and actions of our family can help prevent abortion?_____

_____

10. What can we do in our family to support and encourage chastity?_____

_____

BETWEEN PARENT AND CHILD

As you read your child's text, you will notice a number of personal subjects that are mentioned but not detailed. These are more intimate subjects that are not really suitable for classroom or group discussion for a young teenager. You may wish to discuss them at home with your child in a setting and at a time of your own choosing.

This section is entitled "Between Parent and Child" because your child should learn these things from you, preferably sons from their fathers and daughters from their mothers.

The Vatican document *The Truth and Meaning of Human Sexuality* provides parents with four principles regarding information about sexuality:

1. Each child is a unique and unrepeatable person and must receive individualized formation.
2. The moral dimension must always be part of the explanations.
3. Formation in chastity and timely information regarding sexuality must be provided in the broadest context of education for love.
4. Parents should provide this information with great delicacy, but clearly and at the appropriate time.

Biology of the Reproductive System

It is important to provide necessary biological information to our teens without overwhelming them. They need to be empowered with the truth so that out of curiosity they do not seek other sources for information. As the primary educator, counselor and role model for your child, you are in the best position to talk openly and frankly with your child about the physical, biological details of sexuality. The Church asks us to keep the more intimate aspects of sex education within the family, not in the school or group setting.

Hopefully, you have discussed many of the bodily changes and differences that come with puberty. A parent who will be working through the *Love and Life* program with his teen may want to take the time to review the information that he has already provided. Since education for life is an ongoing process, it never hurts to repeat. You also may find that teens don't remember all that you told them anyway, or they may have received some misinformation since then. Sometimes they have picked up slang terms or disrespectful language regarding sexual parts and actions. Help them to know and use the proper terms so they can show the human body the proper respect.

The following information can be shared with your child, at your own discretion.

Masterpieces of Anatomy: Male and Female

Primary Sex Characteristics

Before any of us was born, God decided whether or not we were to be a man or a woman by assigning us the XX or XY chromosomes. As we developed inside our mother, we acquired additional physical sex characteristics, called primary sex characteristics, which are outward signs of maleness or femaleness.

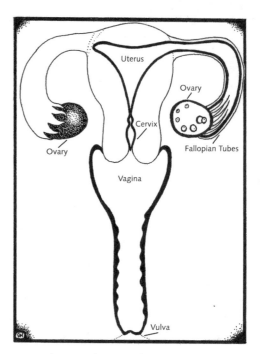

The Female Reproductive System

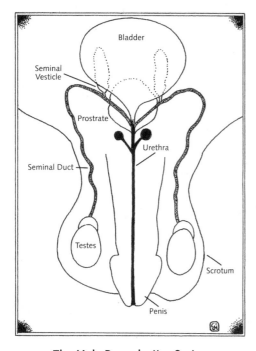

The Male Reproductive System

The primary sex characteristics of a male are the penis, an organ for the transport of urine or semen; and the testes, which produce hormones and sperm. A soft pouch of skin called the scrotum covers the testes. The seminal vesicles are located behind the bladder and prostate gland, and are attached to the top of the seminal ducts. The seminal ducts are the passageways leading from the testes to the urethra.

The primary sex characteristic of a female on the outside of her body is the vulva, which includes protective folds of tissue called labia and the vestibule of the vagina. Over the outside opening of the vagina there is a thin perforated skin called the hymen. The primary sex characteristics inside her body include the two ovaries, which hold ovum (egg) cells and produce hormones; and the uterus, sometimes called the womb, which is a special place where God enters to create new human life. The uterus is a muscular organ that protects and nourishes a developing baby during pregnancy. The muscles of the uterus contract at the end of pregnancy to deliver the baby out into the world. The cervix, the opening at the lower end of the uterus, leads to the vagina, which is the birth canal and the organ designed for sexual intercourse. The fallopian tubes are the passages that extend from the uterus toward the ovaries.

Inside the body there are other less obvious but not less important indications of our maleness or femaleness. Every cell of the human body carries the genetic code that makes a person either male or female.

The brain and the glandular system also differ considerably. Thus, males and females think and act differently. For example, baby girls often learn to talk before the boys, while some boys are great at making noises. Girls often like to dress up in frilly clothes and attract attention, while boys often prefer playing in the mud. Many girls like to dress and redress their dolls; some boys like to play roughly with their toys. The differences become more obvious after puberty. They are all part of the complementary nature of man and woman, as discussed in Chapter 6 of the *Student Guide*.

Puberty—a Time of Changes
After childhood, the differences between boys and girls are more accentuated. The body prepares for adulthood beginning in the preteen years. We refer to this time of life as puberty. It usually occurs between the ages of ten and sixteen (a little later for boys than for girls).

At puberty, the pituitary gland at the base of the brain sends out chemical signals that tell your body to speed up growth. Changes taking place inside your body will make you physically capable of becoming a parent. This is known as fertility. These biological changes that appear at puberty are called your secondary sex characteristics because they weren't present when you were first born.

The shape of a girl's body will change over a few years to the shape of a woman. She often grows in desire to be with her girlfriends and to verbalize every action and thought. She will notice that her moods may easily change; and she must learn to base her actions not on her feelings, but on her conscience and character. Her emerging feminine beauty requires that she learn to dress modestly so as not to distract others.

Boys will notice changes in their appetite as their bones grow longer, shoulders widen, skin toughens and additional hair growth takes place. Their voices also change, becoming deeper. Sometimes the increased influence of the hormone testosterone gives them the desire to be more aggressive, take risks, and crash into each other, as in a football game. A boy's growing strength provides a challenge to conquer his urges to misuse his new powers. Growth in emotional maturity is as important for boys as it is for girls.

Growing from a Girl to a Woman
A girl will notice that her hips become wider, preparing her body to carry a baby during pregnancy. The breasts begin to grow in order that she can nurse a child. Hair growth will occur in the pubic area and

armpits. Inside her body the ovaries begin to produce hormones that prepare her body for motherhood. These hormones trigger the release of the first sign of fertility—cervical mucus. Mild white or clear mucus may be discharged from the vaginal opening at certain times each month, indicating her times of possible fertility. Fertile mucus can nourish the male sperm cells and keep them alive for up to five days. It can also help transport sperm to the ovum (egg). Becoming aware of the monthly changes in the mucus signs will help a girl prepare to understand Natural Family Planning (NFP) later on in marriage. It will also help her understand her mood shifts, which may fluctuate with the monthly hormone changes.

The Menstrual Cycle
Further preparations for biological motherhood are taking place during the fertility cycle. Each month the uterus prepares a cushion-like bloody lining in the event that an ovum is fertilized. Meanwhile, a new ovum matures each month and is released by one of the ovaries. (Ovaries usually alternate ovum production: one ovary releases an ovum one month, and the other the next month.) If no fertilization takes

place, the blood vessels of the cushion-like lining of the uterus close off. The blood and tissue lining the uterus are released through the vagina to the outside of the body. This is called menstruation or a "period", and it occurs about every twenty-eight days.

The menstrual cycle stops temporarily during pregnancy and may also be absent or irregular during breast-feeding. Once a woman reaches her mid-forties or early fifties, God naturally stops the menstrual cycle, when He decides in His own wisdom that a woman should be infertile again. This occurrence is called menopause.

Growing from a Boy to a Man

Boys at puberty grow differently than girls do. Besides growing in size and shape, boys grow more hair on the face and under the arms, as well as on their arms, legs and groin. Inside the male body the testes begin to produce hormones and hundreds of thousands of microscopic sperm cells each day, as well as the liquid —called semen—that helps transport sperm. When sperm production begins during adolescence, a young male is physically capable of becoming a father; but he is usually not emotionally, socially or economically

prepared to be a parent. Sperm production will continue daily for the rest of his life.

This is the beginning of a young man's physical preparation for fatherhood. He must continue to work to develop his character throughout these years of physical development, so that he will be prepared to be a great husband and father if God calls him to the vocation of marriage.

During puberty, boys begin to experience the natural process by which sperm-containing fluid is occasionally released through the penis. This may occur unintentionally during trauma, stress or exhaustion. Sometimes excess seminal fluid is released during a man's sleep. This is called a nocturnal emission or "wet dream".

A young man may also experience an erection, which is a hardening of the penis due to increased blood flow in the area. This can happen due to stress, excitement or boredom, during sleep or for no reason at all—just waking up in the morning. This is normal for boys at puberty, but it often occurs in young boys of any age. If a young man consciously does nothing to cause the erection—for example, it happens in his dreams or when chancing upon stimulating thoughts or materials—there is no sin if he resists any temptations to impure thoughts or actions. If left alone, the erection will go away. Exercise, daily physical activity, and cold showers are also helpful to prevent built-up sexual energies or tension.

This may also be time to discuss the immorality of masturbation, which is covered later in this chapter. Masturbation is never necessary. A young man should respect the sexual powers that God gave him, and use them only within marriage as an act of giving himself in love to his wife. Although there will be times of temptation to physical gratification, sons can be guided to prayer, spiritual reading and apostolic activity. These things can help fill the souls of young men with the desire to please God rather than to gratify themselves.

Emotional Changes

During adolescence, while boys are growing into men and girls are growing into women, there may be times of emotional confusion. Try to help your teen learn emotional self-mastery through proper expression of their feelings. Parents can provide clear guidance and firm discipline to help their teens during these years of fluctuating dependence and independence.

Sexual maturity results from growing in many ways. These are only the physical traits. As our teens learn to accept their new feelings, and their growing bodies, they should channel them into good behavior while developing the virtue of chastity. It is easy, but not good, for a teen to use hormone changes as an excuse to be selfish, difficult to get along with, or moody. Help your teen see these changes as an opportunity to grow in self-mastery.

As our teens learn to love, they should practice relating to others in a kind, not sarcastic, way. They can learn to accept love and understanding and give it to others, especially their parents and brothers and sisters. It is important to teach them to stay pure in mind, heart and body so that it is easier to resist any temptations to hurt or ill-use others. Pray together for an increase in the virtues of purity and chastity, so your teen will have a good chance of becoming sexually mature, as God has planned.

Giving More Detailed Explanations

Instructions for puberty talks in early adolescence from the Vatican document *The Truth and Meaning of Human Sexuality* can help guide parents at this stage:

> **Wonderful are thy works!**
> **Thou knowest me right well;**
> **My frame was not hidden from thee,**
> **when I was being made in secret.**
> **Psalm 139: 14b–15a**

Beginning with the changes which their sons and daughters experience in their bodies, parents are thus bound to give more detailed explanations about sexuality (in an ongoing relationship of trust and friendship) each time girls confide in their mothers and boys in their fathers. This relationship of trust and friendship should have already started in the first years of life. (no. 89)

Another important task for parents is following the gradual physiological development of their daughters and helping them joyfully to accept the development of their femininity in a bodily, psychological and physical sense. Therefore, normally one should discuss the cycles of fertility and their meaning. But it is still not necessary to give detailed explanation about sexual union unless this is explicitly requested. (no. 90)

However, when the question is asked and the timing is right, parents often search for the words to use in explaining the holy and sacred marital act of sexual union. Maybe some of the following words will help you explain it in a reverent way.

> **For thou didst form my**
> **inward parts, thou didst knit me**
> **together in my mother's womb.**
> **Psalm 139:13**

Sexual Intercourse and Conception

God has designed a marvelous plan for the creation of human life. The responsibility for a new human being is so great that children should be conceived within the loving embrace of husband and wife.

In the holy act of marital sexual intercourse, a husband and wife join in bodily union and open themselves to the awesome possibility of generating a new human life. There is no way to describe the conjugal act without in some way diminishing its mystery and sacredness; but in an effort to help you teach your teen, here is an attempt.

During times of physical intimacy, husband and wife prepare for sexual intercourse by tenderly kissing and touching each other. Through this loving preparation, the spouses' genital organs are made ready for union. The husband's erect penis enters the wife's vagina and releases semen. This release is called an ejaculation, but the word cannot begin to express the unity of body and soul experienced by the spouses in this moment.

Semen includes the sperm cells, or sex cells, that are produced in a man's testicles. There are normally millions of tiny sperm cells in one ejaculation. If a couple has sexual intercourse on one of the days of the month when an egg cell is ready for fertilization, the sperm cells swim from the vagina through the cervical opening and through the uterus to meet the ovum in the fallopian tube. Only one sperm enters the ovum, fertilizing the egg. This is part of God's plan to determine the uniqueness of each individual.

Procreation: A New Life Begins

The union of the sperm and the egg is called conception, and it normally takes place in the fallopian tube of the mother. At this moment of conception, a new, unrepeatable and irre-

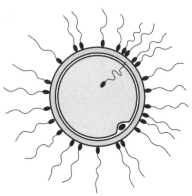

Conception occurs when the sperm fertilizes the egg.

placeable human life begins. Procreation is a three-way cooperative effort: the man and woman contribute the first cells of the body while God creates a soul that will live for eternity.

Conception does not take place every time a couple has sexual intercourse. There are only several days each month when the conditions are right in the woman's body for a new life to begin. Knowing these conditions is called "fertility awareness" and

helps a couple practice Natural Family Planning in order to achieve or avoid a pregnancy.

The Miracle of Life: A Baby Grows
The fertilized egg cell, now called an embryo, divides and multiplies. This growing human being takes a few days to move through the fallopian tube into the mother's womb, where it implants itself in the uterine lining.

In one of the many wonders of life, God provides nourishment for the child through the mother by way of the umbilical cord and placenta, which quickly develop from the child. The placenta clings to the wall of the uterus and transfers nutrition, water and oxygen from the mother's bloodstream to the child's through the umbilical cord. After birth, the umbilical cord is cut and its former attachment place on the baby's abdomen becomes the navel, or belly button.

By six to seven weeks after conception, the baby has grown to almost one inch long. The skeleton is complete, while the arms, legs, body, and face are taking more definite shape.

After the child has been growing inside the mother for about eight to ten weeks, it looks even more like a baby, but is still very small. The child is now called a fetus and is more than one inch long. The baby's heart and brain and other major organs of the body are functioning. This new human life needs only nourishment as its size increases and its little details are perfected. The baby can squint, swallow, move its tongue, and make a fist.

At twelve weeks after conception, the baby is more than three inches long. Fingernails and toenails begin to grow. Arms and legs move, although the movements may be too weak to be felt by the mother. The baby can suck its thumb and swallow the amniotic fluid that surrounds it in a water-filled sack. The baby is still getting nourishment through the umbilical cord. The mother should eat nutritious food and vitamins so her baby can be healthy, too.

The baby inside the womb can be seen by special equipment. Usually, an ultrasound machine can detect the shape and position of the baby, and a pic-

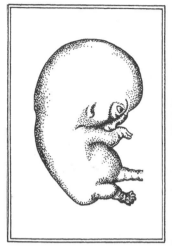

The human embryo at about eight weeks.

The unborn child at about ten weeks.

ture of the baby's shape can be printed. The baby keeps growing inside the mother. The baby's skin is wrinkly from being in the amniotic fluid all the time. For now, the baby gets all its oxygen through the blood in the umbilical cord. In God's design, additional hormones start the mother's mammary glands in her breasts to produce milk so she will be ready to nurse the baby when he is born. At about sixteen weeks after conception, the mother may begin to feel the baby kick her from the inside of the womb. It is wonderful for the mother to feel the baby moving inside her. It's as if they are playing together. It usually doesn't hurt until the baby is so big—at about thirty-six weeks—that he is running out of space to kick inside.

After thirty-eight to forty weeks of gestation, the baby is fully grown and ready to be born. His length is now about twenty inches, and his weight is about seven pounds. The baby's body is rounder and the skin less wrinkled, because the baby has spent his last two months in the uterus gaining weight. The new child is ready for the outside world, yet still dependent on mother for nourishment and care.

If you read Chapter Three of Genesis on original sin, you have a clue that delivering a baby is not easy. "To the woman he said, 'I will greatly multiply your pain in childbearing; in pain you shall bring forth children'" (Genesis 3:16a). Even so, God is with the couple during childbirth, and many techniques can help a mother relax so she can deliver her baby with joy.

How a Baby Is Born

God has designed a special process called labor that usually begins when the nine months of pregnancy are completed. Labor begins when the uterine muscle starts contracting and begins to squeeze the baby in the amniotic sac down into the birth canal to be delivered to the outside world. These muscle contractions are called labor pains. They may hurt the mother like a strong muscle cramp, but she forgets the pain later when she holds her beautiful baby in her arms. The cervix opens up and stretches around the baby, who usually comes out headfirst through the vagina. The baby slides a little farther through the vaginal opening with each contraction of the uterine muscle. After the baby is born, the uterus contracts again and pushes out the placenta.

The baby now starts breathing air through his lungs, and the umbilical cord is cut. The uterus will keep contracting after the baby is born until it returns to the smaller size it was before the pregnancy. The birth of the baby is a joyous occasion. It is often quite moving for a husband to see his wife give birth. It is very exciting for a couple to see their love become alive in a new person, their baby, that even looks like both of them. Two have become one flesh!

As a parent, you may want to share at this time the excitement you felt at the birth of your teen. If he was adopted, you can share the anticipation of his arrival into your family, as well as the special choice God and you and your spouse made to welcome him as your own.

Reproductive Biology Definitions

Although the factual information is not as important as the moral formation, parents are often more confident when the facts are provided. The following definitions may help you explain the material or answer any questions.

cervix—the lower part (neck) of the uterus.

conception—the moment when egg and sperm unite and life begins.

ejaculation—the release of sperm and semen through the penis.

embryo—a developing human being from conception through the first eight to twelve weeks.

erection—when blood vessels inside the penis fill up and increase the size and firmness of the penis.

fallopian tubes—tubal passages extending from the uterus to the ovaries that help transport the egg to the uterus during ovulation; sites of conception.

fertilization—the moment when a male sperm enters a female ovum.

fetus—a developing child from the third month of gestation until birth.

genetic—inherited by offspring from parents as passed on through the genes.

genitals—the organs designed by God to help generate life; the penis and vagina, the organs for sexual intercourse.

gestation—the period during which a child develops in the womb.

hormone—a chemical compound produced by the glands and carried to the site of action by the bloodstream; hormones influence the growth and function of various parts of the body.

hymen — the thin protective layer of skin covering the outside opening of the vagina in a female virgin.

labia—folds of skin in the female that enclose the opening to the vagina, the clitoris and the opening of the urethra.

maturity—the state of being fully developed.

ovaries—the female glands that produce hormones and contain ovum in which the ova reach maturity.

ovum—a mature egg cell.

penis—the male organ that provides for the release of urine and semen.

pituitary gland—the gland located at the base of the brain which produces hormones affecting growth, metabolism and other bodily functions.

placenta—the organ that nourishes the developing baby in the womb.

pregnancy—the usual period of nine months, during which a developing fetus is carried within the uterus; it begins at conception and ends at birth.

prostate gland—a chestnut-shaped body surrounding the urethra in the male; it contributes a secretion to semen.

puberty—the stage of life when fertility begins.

pubis—the region in the lower part of the abdomen, near the genitals.

scrotum—a soft pouch of skin on the outside of the male body that contains the testes.

semen—the fluid that helps transport sperm, the male reproductive cells.

seminal duct—the canal that conveys semen to the urethra.

seminal vesicle—in the male, bags attached to the back of the bladder opening into the seminal duct.

sexual intercourse—the physical union of the male and female sexual organs.

sperm—male reproductive cells produced in the testes.

testes—the male paired gland that produces sperm and reproductive cells; also referred to as *testicles*.

umbilical cord—ropelike tissue connecting the fetus with the placenta, so that nourishment may be carried to and wastes removed from the fetus.

uterus—the muscular organ that holds the developing baby during pregnancy; also referred to as the womb.

vagina—the birth canal and female organ for sexual intercourse.

vas deferens—the tubes through which sperm cells are sent from the testes to the urethra.

vulva—external genital area of the female including labia and vestibule of vagina.

Other Questions Teens May Ask

If you have an inquisitive teen, continue to answer his questions truthfully and respectfully in light of God's plan. Perversions and abuses of sex do not need to be explained in detail, so use discretion. As much as possible protect the innocence and purity of your child.

Can You Get Pregnant without "Going All the Way"?

Let's begin that answer by reminding our teens that virginity is a beautiful and priceless gift. Instead of seeing "how far we can go", we should be thinking of how pure we should be to know and do God's will for our happiness.

In addition to reviewing the standard biological facts, another important point to bring up at home, if your teens need it, is that a pregnancy can occur anytime a sperm travels through the mucus to meet an ovum. This means it *is* possible for a couple to conceive a child even when the penis has not entered the vagina. If semen reaches mucus outside the vagina, it can travel through the cervical mucus from the outside to the inside of the vagina.

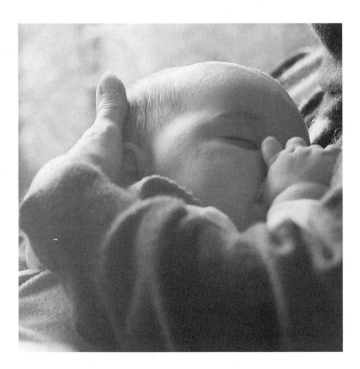

Is It OK to Have Other Kinds of Sex Play Outside of Marriage?

No. Remember that people are not toys to be played with, and God designed sexual pleasure to be part of love-giving and life-giving in marriage. **It is wrong to play around with any type of sexually arousing activity outside of marriage.** Besides being dangerous for the unmarried, mutual sex play or "fooling around", as well as oral sex play, is immoral even if no actual intercourse takes place. The distorted information available through the media today compels us to instruct our teens clearly on the immorality of these acts. Oral sex, mutual masturbation and withdrawal are violations of chastity and forms of lust.

To properly reflect God's love, all sexually pleasurable activity should be within marriage as a preparation for the personal union of sexual intercourse. God designed the bodies of man and woman to give and to receive one another in the flesh-to-flesh, person-to-person, face-to-face act of sexual intercourse, in a loving embrace uniting the genital organs. The goodness and dignity of sexual acts are protected when those actions are directed toward the unitive and procreative ends of marriage.

In other words sexual pleasure is not to be sought as an end in itself either inside or outside of marriage. Sexual pleasure is a gift from God that properly results from natural sexual intercourse between husband and wife.

What's So Bad about Abortion?

God is the author of life, therefore no one has the right to kill an innocent human being. The Vatican guidelines for parents suggest that the immoral nature of abortion be gradually explained before adolescence. If you have not previously discussed it, now is the time to explain that life begins at conception and that the teachings against abortion are based on our reverence for life. You can also go over the teachings in the *Catechism*, as referenced in Chapter 22 of the *Student Guide*.

Questions about Birth Control

When the topic of birth control comes up, Catholic parents have a duty to present the authentic teaching of the Church.

Perhaps you do not accept or understand this teaching yourself. Then why not take this opportunity to learn about it, along with your teen. It's better to learn now than never! Failing to present this critical teaching could place your child in danger of losing his purity and of failing to find true happiness in marriage. Do your best to understand it and pass it on to the next generation.

> As regards sterilization and contraception, these should not be discussed before adolescence and only in conformity with the teaching of the Catholic Church. Therefore, the moral, spiritual and health values of methods for the natural regulation of fertility will be emphasized, at the same time indicating the dangers and ethical aspects of the artificial methods. In particular, the substantial and deep difference between natural methods and artificial methods will be shown, both with regard to respect for God's plan for marriage as well as for achieving "the total reciprocal self-giving of husband and wife" and openness to new life. (TM, no. 137)

How Do I Explain Birth Control to My Son or Daughter?

Artificial birth control, abortion and infanticide have been around a very long time and were commonplace in the ancient world. From its beginning, the Church has always taught that these practices are wrong. Artificial birth control is contraception. *Contraception* means "against conception". Contraception works against nature. The Catholic Church teaches us that contraception is wrong because it is not only against conception and nature, but also against God, love, women, children and marital unity. Contraception, in any form, comes between the couple during their sexual union and prevents them from fully becoming one.

Contraception also interferes with God's design that sexual intercourse is potentially life-giving.

> There is an inseparable connection, willed by God, that is unable to be broken by man on his own, between the unitive meaning [lovegiving] and the procreative meaning [lifegiving] of the conjugal act. Indeed by its intimate nature, the conjugal act, while most closely uniting husband and wife, makes them apt for the generation of new lives, according to laws inscribed in the very being of man and woman.

> By safeguarding these two aspects, the unitive and procreative, the conjugal act preserves in its fullness the sense of true mutual love and its ordination toward man's most high calling to parenthood. (*Humanae Vitae*, no. 12)

Remember when we talked about conception? Conception occurs when the sperm cell from the father meets the egg cell of the mother. A contraceptive either tries to block the sperm from meeting the egg, or the egg from being released from the ovary, or a fertilized egg from implanting in the uterus. A person using contraception is trying to block out God's power to create a new human life while at the same time engaging in the act that God designed to transmit life. Contraceptive sex is like eating food and vomiting it before it can be digested. The person who does this is trying to enjoy the taste of food while preventing the consequences of digestion. We call such behavior an eating *disorder* because it is against the way our bodies are made. Disordered behaviors, which are contrary to our natures, do us harm. But in the case of using contraception, which is a sexual disorder, two people are harmed. When a couple uses contraception, they enjoy the pleasures of sexual intercourse without accepting the union and procreation that can result.

Just look at the consequences. The divorce rate in this country has skyrocketed since contraception became widespread, but many people still aren't making the connection. According to the U.S. Census Bureau statistics in 2003, 43 percent of first marriages fail, and the divorce rate is higher for second and third marriages, making the average divorce rate near 50 percent. On the other hand, according to studies done by Natural Family Planning (NFP) providers such as the Family of the Americas and the Couple to Couple League, the divorce rate for couples who use NFP is less than 5 percent, with most studies reporting less than 2 percent over twenty years. There is a huge difference between marriages with contraception and marriages with NFP! We don't know all the reasons or causes for these big differences, but it speaks highly of God's plan for marriage.

Additional Questions on Contraception

Parents, if your teen is additionally curious or has been exposed to more information on contraception, the following specifics may clarify the facts or relieve curiosity. It is not information that all teens need to know right away.

Barriers to Love and Life
Some contraceptive devices block the sperm from meeting the egg. They act as a barrier or fortress to separate the man's gift of fertility from the woman's gift of fertility. There can be no total gift of self when these devices are used. You may have heard of the condom, which is a rubber sheath that men place over their sexual organ to trap the sperm released during ejaculation. Another barrier contraceptive is a diaphragm, a device that a woman places inside her vagina to block the sperm from reaching the egg. Contraceptives make the sexual act unnatural and can even make it unpleasurable. The marital act should be a time of closeness and intimacy, not a time for spouses to "protect themselves" from each other. Married love is supposed to be a free and unconditional gift of one's whole self to the other. Barrier contraceptives cause division, not unity.

The Church's teaching against contraception makes sense. First, the last thing we usually do when we wish to touch someone tenderly is to put gloves on! Second, when we contracept, we defend ourselves against our spouse. Usually, we only defend ourselves against enemies. In effect, then, when we contracept, we see our spouse as a threat.

What about Chemical Contraceptives?
Contraceptive chemicals are even more than a barrier to conception. Contraceptive chemicals go into a woman's body and change her hormones so that she will not release an egg each month. It is wrong to use drugs or devices to harm or destroy the natural

function of a healthy reproductive system. Since this action of stopping ovulation does not always work, most chemical contraceptives have a backup mechanism that makes the woman's body hostile to the sperm cells and hostile to a new human life if it is conceived anyway. These contraceptive chemicals prevent the embryo from implanting and growing in the womb. These chemicals automatically cause an abortion before the mother even knows she is pregnant. Some refer to the chemical contraceptives as abortifacients because they cause an instant abortion. In this category would be the birth control pill that a woman takes orally each day of her cycle, a depo-provera shot that she gets every couple months from her doctor or clinic and a hormone implant under the skin or patch on the skin.

Another negative effect of chemical contraceptives is on the woman herself. Because they interfere with the delicate workings of the female endocrine system, chemical contraceptives, especially when used over a long period of time, can be harmful to a woman's health and can impair her ability to conceive a child later on.

Unfortunately, many doctors promote chemical contraceptives with their female patients because they assume everyone has adopted a casual view of sexual activity. A new group of doctors, however, has taken a stand against contraception. They are registered with an organization called One More Soul. These doctors want to practice responsible medicine, which respects both nature and God's plan, whether or not it is popular.

What Is Natural Family Planning and How Is It Different from Contraception?

The Church teaches that contraception is wrong because it thwarts the very purposes of sexual intercourse—the union of the spouses and the procreation of children. If a married couple has serious reasons for spacing children or limiting the size of their family, then the Church permits the use of Natural Family Planning (NFP).

NFP is not a method of contraception. NFP is fertility awareness. God has made human fertility in such a way that not every act of sexual intercourse results in pregnancy. During the course of her menstrual cycle, the woman has natural periods of fertility and infertility. After a certain age, a woman's periods of fertility cease altogether. Knowing when fertility occurs can help a married couple either to achieve or avoid pregnancy. Pregnancy can be achieved by engaging in sexual intimacy during the woman's fertile time. Pregnancy can be avoided by abstaining from sexual intimacy during the woman's fertile time.

Abstinence during times of fertility is not the same as contraception. A contracepting couple is trying to enjoy the pleasures of sexual intimacy while destroying the life-giving power of the sexual act. It represents a lack of respect for the gift of fertility, usually that of the woman, and leads to the attitudes that sex is only for pleasure and that children conceived in spite of contraception are "accidents". Couples practicing periodic abstinence, on the other hand, retain their respect for the life-giving power of sexual intercourse. During times of sexual intimacy they do not try to harm or hinder their fertility and are open to the awesome possibility of a new life being created. When a couple has decided to abstain from sex for reasons they have agreed upon, they look for nonphysical ways to show their love; and because abstinence requires some sacrifice, it builds up the spouses in virtue and mutual respect.

There are many times during the normal course of married life when it is imprudent or even impossible for spouses to have sexual relations—during times of sickness or absence, for example. Likewise, sexual intercourse during times of infertility is also a normal part of married life because times of infertility are naturally more common than those of fertility.

Some people have accepted the contraceptive mentality out of fear that they cannot practice self-control, or that God would not provide for their families as He has promised. Others are misinformed about the true nature of contraception and NFP.

Unlike contraception, natural methods of family planning are not based on fear, but on faith in God and His design for nature. The modern natural methods (sympto-thermal and ovulation) are highly effective, even during irregular cycles, menopause or breast-feeding. They also provide many personal and spiritual benefits to the married couple.

With these accurate and reliable methods of NFP, there is no need to suffer the side effects, inconveniences or sinfulness of contraception. Through the wisdom of our Church, we can truly experience God's love and life in our families. NFP is a sign of respect for God's Lordship in our lives.

Why Is Sterilization Wrong?

Voluntary sterilization for birth control purposes is a permanent surgical destruction of one's healthy fertility, usually through vasectomy or tubal ligation. It is a sin against the sixth commandment regarding marriage, as well as the fifth commandment regarding mutilation of one's healthy body. Sterilization is a destructive act against God's creation of man and woman.

Fertility is one of the most sacred gifts God has given us. By sterilizing themselves, people reject this gift and harm their body. If we really think about it,

sterilization is a form of despair. It says, "I will never be able to control my sex drives." This may be a misunderstanding of human self-mastery, or a direct acceptance of lust. It may be an outright rejection of God's loving action in one's life, or ignorance of God's real loving plan for human sexual expression. Either way, it is harmful to sex in marriage and works against continued growth in sexual maturity and holiness. Fertility is to be respected because it is a great privilege that God has entrusted to us.

However, if a reproductive organ is diseased and must be surgically removed to save a person's life or health, it is acceptable to do so, even if such removal indirectly results in sterilization.

Children Are a Gift from God

> Fecundity is a gift, an *end of marriage,* for conjugal love naturally tends to be fruitful. A child . . . springs from the very heart of that mutual giving, as its fruit and fulfillment. (*Catechism of the Catholic Church,* no. 2366)

Children are a gift from God, so it's hard to believe how popular contraception has become over the last forty years. Many people just don't know God's plan for married love is so wonderful. Many don't realize the joy they are missing by not having more children. The worldwide organization Planned Parenthood International spends billions of dollars convincing people that children are burdensome, that contraception and abortion are good and necessary. Unfortunately, they have been successful in promoting their lies to people all over the world, including many Christians and Catholics. High schools and colleges, both public and private, teach students about birth control devices and chemicals as if they were healthful and normal.

Contraception is not good for one's health because it causes a normal, working reproductive system to malfunction. Contraception is not good for one's emotional health because it allows a couple to try to change the meaning of the sexual act. Contraception is never good for one's spiritual health, because it blocks out God from a couple's love life and turns it into a mere sex life. They miss out on the grace that can make their whole marriage a participation in the divine. Couples who resist the sin of contraception and embrace the teachings of the Church will receive the grace from God needed in their state of life. They will also receive the fulfillment that comes from planning their family in cooperation with God.

Disordered Sexual Behavior

These issues can be discussed with Unit 4, Chapter 21 of the *Student Guide*, or when the topic arises in home discussion.

Masturbation

Masturbation is a misuse of our sexual powers. It is the deliberate stimulation of one's own genital organs to derive sexual pleasure. Masturbation is treating oneself as a sex object, or using one's body as a toy. Masturbation is an immature and degrading act that relieves sexual tension by succumbing to sexual urges when there is no union, no life giving, or no love giving possible. This is contrary to the purposes of the genital organs, which are procreation and the union of husband and wife.

Our Church teaches that "masturbation is an intrinsically and seriously disordered act" (*Vatican Declaration on Sexual Ethics*). It violates the "full sense of mutual self-giving and human procreation in the context of true love".

To intentionally stimulate the sexual organs of another person to whom one is not married is sometimes called mutual masturbation, sometimes called "petting". This is also an immoral use of one's sex-

ual powers. God designed this kind of affection for married couples to prepare one another's bodies for the marital embrace. Such behavior is inappropriate outside of marriage and leads to sexual frustration.

Oral sex and anal sex are forms of mutual masturbation. Both actions introduce the digestive system to the reproductive system and are immoral because they misuse parts of the body and replace true sexual union. The genitals are designed to help generate life; they are naturally clean and are not made to be connected to the germ-laden or bacteria-laden ends of the digestive system. Both oral and anal sex cause disease and damage the body.

The delicate topic of masturbation is best discussed in the privacy of one's own home, or with a priest in the confessional, not in the classroom or in mixed groups. For this reason, your child's text does not include details on this subject. It merely lists it as a violation or sin against God's plan for sexuality. As a parent, you should address the issue so the child will be prepared to resist temptations. Be aware that your sons may need this information sooner than your daughters.

Some psychologists claim that masturbation is normal. By this they mean it is common. However, lying is common also, but that does not make it right. Masturbation focuses physical sexual arousal on oneself, rather than directing that focus on love for a spouse in the embrace of Christian marriage, as in God's design. Masturbation is the opposite of God's design for sexual expression. Some secular sex educators falsely teach that masturbation is equal to abstinence and a good alternative to premarital sex for single people. First of all, it is not the same as abstinence; and second, masturbation does not help a person practice abstinence from sexual intercourse. On the contrary, it has the opposite effect, by stirring up sexual desires and creating frustration. Masturbation is habit-forming and makes the practice of chastity extremely difficult.

Teenagers, especially young men, can easily fall into masturbation out of weakness, immaturity or curiosity. It is important as a parent to guide them to good habits and a good confessor who can help them overcome this sinful behavior. If a young person thinks masturbation is just normal and acceptable, the natural tendency is to keep doing it. Yet the habit of masturbation can cause serious psychological and sexual problems. It works against the development of self-control and it can undermine true sexual enjoyment later on in a marriage. A good prayer life and frequent reception of the sacraments can provide the grace necessary to avoid this sin.

Cohabitation

A man and woman who live together like husband and wife but without the commitment of marriage sin against both modesty and chastity as taught in the 6th and 9th commandments. Though cohabitation has become very common in Western societies, the trend is doing serious harm to men and women and their capacity for loving and faithful family life. Many people justify cohabitation with the excuse that they are checking out their partner's suitability for marriage. Though cohabiting couples seem to benefit from some of the goods of a shared life, they lack the sacramental grace that is needed to make the relationship work. People who do not understand the objective benefits of marriage vows have fallen for the deception that cohabitation reduces the chances of divorce. But according to a university study of thirty thousand couples, 80 percent of those who lived together before marriage broke up within the first ten years. Marriage after cohabitation also has the highest adultery rate. If someone does not respect God's plan for marriage when he is single, how likely is he to respect it after he is married?

A man and woman who live together without the trust that comes from making a commitment often do not really get to know each other. Sociological studies on cohabiting couples have shown that they have difficulty being honest with one another about their feelings or about the relationship because they realize they are only being tested for

acceptability. Couples reported that they couldn't identify their feelings of confusion and never spoke about it because they were afraid of losing their sex partner. Dr. Joyce Brothers has demonstrated that cohabiting women, in particular, tend to be in denial that no commitment has been made. They often act like wives and try to build a common life for the couple. The men, on the other hand, rarely reciprocate. In the absence of formal vows, they feel neither the desire nor the duty to treat the woman as anything more than a mistress. They may learn about one another physically, but cohabiting couples suffer great emotional and psychological losses to their human capacity to live the true fullness of life. Men and women were not made for experimentation or trial runs when it comes to love and sex.

Although checking out people's compatibility works during chaste dating, it backfires in a cohabitation situation. Sexual desires confuse the person about the differences between love and lust. The hormone oxytocin, which the body releases during sexual excitement, creates a bond between two sexually active persons that can confuse them as to the reality of the relationship. It's then very difficult to know if the other person is in love with you, or in love with sex. Or perhaps they are in love with themselves and are using you for their sexual pleasure. "Testing" compatibility is not fair, because human hearts are sensitive and vulnerable. It's ironic that some of the same people who won't test their shampoo on animals will try to "test" false intimacy on humans.

By choosing cohabitation, the couple can destroy a possible marriage that could have worked before they have a chance to learn about real love. Cohabitation is a mockery of marriage. It does not prepare a couple for marriage; it is a life of sin, which is the opposite of love. The best thing a cohabiting couple can do to test their relationship is to live apart for a year and stop sexual activity. Chaste dating will help them see one another more clearly before they make a lifetime decision. The best preparation for marriage is prayer, frequent confession and Communion, and an active life with family and friends.

Pornography

Pornography is any written, visual or audio material that displays or describes sexual organs or sexual acts for the purpose of arousing sexual desire. By arousing sexual urges as ends in themselves, these offenses against chastity pervert the meaning and purpose of sexual love and do grave injury to the dignity of its participants, making them the objects or the slaves of base appetites. Participating in any way with pornography is a serious sin.

What Harm Can Pornography Do?

Pornography immerses its participants in a fantasy world of sex without human love. These materials harm the person by enslaving him to lust and by planting in the imagination memories and attitudes that can undermine one's capacity for a happy marriage. Any exposure to pornography begins the separation of sex from love and marriage. Continued exposure to sexually arousing scenes in movies and television shows, sex-oriented magazines or websites and suggestive songs make it difficult, if not impossible, to achieve sexual maturity.

Adolescent values and morals are not secure or mature; they are still being formed. To malform a young person's conscience and subconscious with erotic material is a serious offense against God. A person who watches, reads and listens to sexual immorality will begin to believe that lust is unconquerable, if not normal and acceptable. When the time comes to make a difficult moral decision, what foundation will he be able to stand upon?

Pornography can develop expectations and fantasies by which a person can judge his spouse's "performance". This cheapens and abuses one's spouse. Sexual expression in marriage is designed to renew the commitment to the marriage vows. Although God designed the act to be pleasurable, pleasure is a side effect and a gift, not the goal. When the marital act is compared with pornographic images, it loses its meaning.

To sum up, pornography has many negative effects:

1. It lowers our standard of propriety and decency.
2. It trivializes human sexuality.
3. It promotes and engenders disordered sexual behavior.
4. It depersonalizes sex and sells sex as an end in itself.
5. It removes the importance of responsibility and commitment from sexual intimacy.
6. It separates love and sex, giving sex a higher value than love.
7. It creates wrong and misleading impressions and fantasies that can harm a loving marriage.
8. It subconsciously creates a perverse understanding of a future wife's or husband's sexuality and physical attractiveness.
9. It celebrates lust and destroys and makes a mockery of self-control.

10. It sets "body beautiful" standards for men and women, with no recognition of inner beauty or moral character.
11. It exploits men, women and children who, often out of desperation, allow themselves to be used.
12. It degrades human persons by reducing them to mere sex objects.

It is extremely important for parents to teach their children to be vigilant in avoiding pornography. Custody of the eyes, which is looking away from immodest commercials or billboards, is a beginning. Teach your sons from a young age to be quick with the remote control to flash off immodest shows and commercials. Reiterate the importance of turning their eyes from billboards and print ads that exhibit immodesty and walking out on movies that are indecent. Filtering your Internet access is essential. Teach them to flee from pornography as quickly as possible. Addictions to pornography and sexual disorders have become a grave problem for both single and married people. Be serious in teaching your teens to avoid viewing impure movies and pictures. Just as you would not put a little poison in their food, teach them not to allow it into their soul.

Homosexual Activity

In God's magnificent design, men and women complement one another. Man finds his completion in woman, and woman in man. The male and female bodies are designed to join together in the one-flesh union, blessed with the graces of the Sacrament of Matrimony. A same-sex relationship cannot result in sexual union. Homosexual activity involves feeble and degrading efforts to get sexual gratification that can never be fulfilling. A homosexual relationship is futile and can never be fruitful in the transmission of new life. No unity or procreation is possible in a sexual relationship between two people of the same sex, therefore attempts at sexual pleasure in homosexual activity result in frustration, physical and emotional harm and despair.

As the secular media proclaims homosexual rights and the current discussion of AIDS becomes alarming, today's teens seem to have more questions concerning homosexuality. In the search for identity during adolescence, your child should be guided in this area with clear knowledge that homosexuality is not just another choice of lifestyle. The teaching of Scripture is clear: "You shall not lie with a male as with a woman; it is an abomination" (Leviticus 18:22).

The Church has provided clear guidance for us in this area. The Vatican document *On the Pastoral Care of Homosexuals* corrects the false notion that homosexuality is "neutral or even good". The pastoral statement clarifies the difference between homosexual orientation and homosexual activity. The homosexual tendency or urge, while not sinful in itself, is nevertheless a "tendency ordered toward an intrinsic moral evil; and thus the inclination itself must be seen as an objective disorder" (no. 3).

While the Church is called to pastoral attention and concern for homosexuals, it is necessary to teach clearly that the living out of this orientation in homosexual activity is not morally acceptable. The document reminds us of the Church's constant teaching: "It is only in the marital relationship that the use of the sexual faculty can be morally good" (no. 7).

Persons suffering from homosexual urges are human beings, capable of self-control, who should acknowledge this condition as a special cross. As is normal for any human person, God permits crosses in our lives that are hard to bear. Crosses allow us an opportunity to grow closer to God and become stronger as a person: "As in every conversion from evil, the abandonment of homosexual activity will require a profound collaboration of the individual with God's liberating grace" (no. 11).

Because of the acceptance of homosexual relationships in the secular culture, some teens may wonder if a simple attraction or deep friendship with a person of the same sex means that they have homosexual tendencies. Assure them that this is most often not the case. Friendship and admiration do not have to lead to romance or sexual attraction. Even a person with a perceived homosexual orientation is called to practice chastity out of faithfulness to God. Feelings can always be mastered through one's reason and actions with the help of God's grace.

If there is additional concern about homosexuality in your family, you may need more guidance. A Catholic organization that can help persons overcome homosexual temptations is Courage. Father John Harvey founded Courage, and its goal is to help Catholic homosexuals live chastely according to the Church's moral teaching. Members have a support system for developing interior chastity, which is even holier than mere abstinence. More information on Courage can be found on their website. A support group for parents, called EnCourage, is also available.

The recent decades of education for gender neutrality have taken their toll on the masculinity of men and femininity of women. Gender confusion in the culture has turned into a new problem of sexual identity disorder. On the other hand, scientific studies have not concluded the debate as to whether homosexuality is learned, biological or both. Therefore, the good news is that parents are not helpless when it comes to maximizing the likelihood of their child growing up heterosexual. The clinical expertise and professional research of Dr. Joseph Nicolosi can offer

practical advice for parents who may be concerned about a possible homosexual orientation in their children. Nicolosi's book, *A Parent's Guide to Preventing Homosexuality*, reveals his research on the antecedents of homosexuality. His guide also educates and encourages parents with practical advice on helping children develop a secure gender identity, such as sports competition and opportunities for interior toughness to help young boys develop their masculinity. He also teaches parents how to recognize behavior that is counterproductive. Nicolosi's teachings are not homophobic, but commonsense clinical advice for parents who wish to lay a foundation for a sound heterosexual identity in their children.

Boys and girls in their preteen years should have good relationships with men and women of character who can serve as role models. They need fathers, uncles, neighbors, scout leaders or coaches to admire. They also need good relationships with mothers, sisters and female friends. Wholesome relationships lead to a wholesome sexuality.

Technological Human Reproduction

Chapter 21 of the *Student Guide* addresses both contraception and technological reproduction. Many questions may arise that can best be answered by you at home. Read Chapter 21 with your teen and allow some of the following information to help you.

The dignity of the human person requires that we do not treat each other as objects to be manufactured as one person sees fit, nor to be disposed of as another sees fit. To protect against this, every human being should be conceived within the loving embrace of husband and wife. Trying to generate human beings in laboratories is trying to "play God". Because we are capable of doing something, does not mean we should do it. Human beings must not be treated as commodities to be manufactured nor by-products to be thrown away.

Artificial insemination of a female ovum with a male sperm outside of sexual intercourse, or the creation of "test-tube babies", or even the attempted cloning of a human being may seem desirable for childless couples. However, it raises serious moral questions. When experimentation is involved, nine of ten newly conceived lives are destroyed at the hands of a medical technician, causing hundreds of thousands of deaths of the tiniest babies. Hundreds of thousands more embryos are left frozen in storage to be used or disposed of at the parents' or scientists' will. Moreover, children conceived artificially have a higher rate of birth defects. God's plan is for a child to be created as a result of a loving sexual union. Scientific efforts address only the physical process of conception. They ignore the intrinsic connection between love giving and life giving as a part of the marital act. Artificial insemination takes away the unitive dimension of the sex act and distorts the procreative dimension.

There are many moral technical procedures that can assist a married couple's fertility to help the natural acts of union and conception. These respect the union of husband and wife as well as allow the conception to take place within that physical union. One ethical institution that specializes in reproductive health is the Pope Paul VI Institute in Omaha, Nebraska. Catholic bioethics organizations and Natural Family Planning groups can also provide referrals to medical practioners that use moral means to help infertile couples.

A human life is always a gift from God. It is not a "right" of the couple to conceive a child, even if they want children. The child is not an object to be owned, nor is the generation of human life ours to control. This teaching is often difficult for childless couples to accept. The Church's position is not insensitive, but it is consistent with respect for the dignity of human life and procreation. The basic dignity of the human person keeps us from using inappropriate means, even to carry out the desires of a loving couple. The underlying principle is God's love for us, and the dignity that His love imparts to each person who is created.

While the Catholic Church cares deeply for couples suffering from sterility, it is assigned by God to protect the integrity of love and life. It is also possible that being childless or adopting children can be a part of God's plan for our holiness. Additional teaching on the issues of artificial generation of life can be found in the *Catholic Catechism,* in *Donum Vitae* (a Vatican document on technological reproduction) or *Interventions upon Human Procreation* by the United States Conference of Catholic Bishops.

> **The human being must be respected — as a person — from the very first instant of his existence. (Instruction on Respect for Human Life in Its Origin and the Dignity of Procreation, 1987)**

EDUCATION FOR A LIFETIME

Raising children to be holy and good is an arduous task because there are many forces against us. It is possible to raise children to be respectful and courteous, to strive for high ideals and reach them. It is possible, though challenging, to raise children who will withstand peer pressure and act with honesty and integrity. To live in pursuit of God's will for them, they must not only develop character traits and virtues, but also face up to their mistakes. Teens and parents all make mistakes, some more serious than others. But when we know where we are heading, the road becomes clearer.

Developing a sense of humor and fun can help bring the joy back to parenting. We need joyful memories to help us face the trials and pain that will naturally come our way.

Our adolescents face many challenges in growing to maturity. They need all the help and support we can offer. They need to learn to face their responsibilities. They need moral guidance. They need our prayers. We must never give up—just as Jesus has never given up on us, going all the way to the Cross. There are sacrifices we will be called on to make for our teens—our time, our energy, our patience and our strength to stand firm when it would be easier to give up and give in. Our love should stand firm, just as God's love stands firm. His grace is there to support us. All we need do is ask in prayer.

As parents we have the challenge of passing on to our children the morals that will carry them through a lifetime. We can do this through:

- Love and affirmation
- Teaching by example
- Keeping communication lines open
- Giving good directions
- Setting limits that eliminate some of the pressure
- Receiving encouragement from the Church and other parents

Love

It is important that we let our young people know in every way that we love them, and that God loves them, unconditionally.

If our teens don't experience unconditional love from us as parents, it is more difficult for them to understand what God's unconditional love is like. Our children learn about the love of God as they experience our parental love. This, along with the formation we provide in the Faith, can create in them a love for God and for themselves. Our unconditional love helps them believe in God and in themselves. Our love and encouragement to do good helps them fight peer pressure. We can show them that it's all right to be different if it means doing the right thing.

We show them by our example that love is patient and kind, not jealous or boastful, not proud or selfish.

It is impossible to show a child too much of God's love. A spoiled child has received too many substitutes for love. We must let children know that our love will back them in their decisions to follow God's plan, even if they are rejected by their friends.

Showing our love is not always an easy task. Teenagers are moody and unpredictable as they move from the simplicity of childhood to the independence of being a mature adult. If we show our understanding and patience, these trials of growing up will pass, and a mature young Christian adult will be formed.

Sincere affection is very important. Teenagers need to be hugged, just like everyone else. This may seem awkward at first, especially on a day when you don't even like your teenager, but you as a parent will need to take the initiative. We all need a pat on the back and an affirming hug once in a while. Don't send them out into the world looking for the love and affection they are missing at home. The result is insecure, immature and destructive relationships.

Our teenagers need us for emotional strength. Even if they spend much of their time with their friends, our children need us desperately during adolescence. Remember how some of the loneliest moments of the teen years are spent:

- At the school dance, where there are hundreds of people but no who one cares enough to ask you to dance
- In the middle of a big party, where you aren't sure who your real friends are
- While staying home "to do homework" on the weekends because you don't care for the games people play at these social gatherings

Our cultural dating patterns and high school status awards, such as "Prom Queen" and "Valentine Sweetheart", seem to reward those who are already glorified with looks and popularity. The other 80 percent of youth need to find their productive place in society. We can help their sense of self-worth by our love, encouragement and emotional support. Teenagers are hungry for our attention, for someone to feel close to who is interested in them. We need to be there with love!

Teach by Example

Let teens see the love in your marriage.

"Why wait till marriage?" the young teen wonders. "My mom and dad don't even seem to like each other."

It is extremely important for children to witness the love of their parents. A wise saying goes: *The greatest gift a father can give to his children is to love their mother.*

Do our children see marriage as good? Do they see that we can work through our trials and grow closer? Do we spend time together as a couple? Are we really sharing our lives as a couple?

By our example, children can see that marriage is more than just the passion they see on television. It is a deeply committed relationship. Our children do not need to see our passionate displays of affection, but they can see our love in our actions and attitudes toward one another. They can see the affection we express. Our example is their marriage education. Children hear how their father talks about women and how their mother regards men, and these impressions will shape their attitudes.

We can show our love in front of our children by:

- Doing favors for one another
- Showing a genuine concern for each other's feelings
- Making sacrifices with a sense of joy, or at least without complaining
- Telling our children how we appreciate our spouse
- Giving one another encouragement
- Showing courtesy and giving compliments
- Being considerate of others' needs
- Saying "I love you!"
- Praying together

Better than any book, our example will show teens that love is patient, kind and self-sacrificing.

How Single Parents Set Examples

Single parents face extra challenges. Recovering from death, separation or divorce often can add strength to a parent-child bond. This is not always the case, however. It is critical to take the time to listen carefully to a child's feelings about this loss. Sharing these feelings will help to strengthen this bond.

Divorced parents can display Christian qualities of love through their attitude toward and discussion of their former spouse. Children sense these quickly, and can see bitterness, anger and hatred, or forgiveness, acceptance and a loving attitude. It is unfair to destroy a child's image of the other parent or of marriage in general. We need to help them to make a better vocational choice themselves and guide them with the strength and truth of God's love.

Single parents who date have a special calling to set a good example for their adolescents, who will learn from their parents' conduct such things as

- Attitudes toward dating relationships
- Behavior on a date
- How to dress
- How late to stay out

A double standard doesn't pass with teenagers. They will imitate what they see their parents do more than listen to what they say.

What Example Do We Set in Our Handling of Daily Situations?

Do we practice temperance? Overindulgence in any area is not good spiritually or physically. Moderation in the use of food, alcohol, prescription drugs and luxuries is an important example to set. We must keep working on our own development. If our own lives are out of order, it becomes difficult to teach self-control to our young. We set the example!

Keep Communication Lines Open

If we have been open and honest in communicating with our children throughout childhood, things do not need to change at puberty. Parents who have answered all the little questions along the way can keep their teens coming to them for sound, truthful information. Parents who have been silent in the past can still open the avenues now.

One of the best times to talk to teens is before bed at night. Vulnerability seems to set in at day's end. Be a good listener, even when it is tiring. Take a nap if needed, so you are prepared to be open to the possibility.

We need to be understanding of romances and crushes. Our child's first feelings of attraction to a member of the opposite sex are an occasion to let him or her know this is normal and good. But parents can help their teen to recognize those feelings for what they are—first attractions, not true love.

Opportunities arise every day to initiate a discussion with your teen about attitudes toward sexuality. Discussing events in newspapers or on television programs and in movies can help to give perspective, substance and shape to morals. A simple question at a commercial break or the end of a program can develop into a great little conversation.

Set Family Standards for Purity

The following story can provide assistance you may need for parental screening to help keep your teen's mind as pure as possible:

Brownies with a Difference

Many parents are hard-pressed to explain to their youth why some music, movies, books, and magazines are not acceptable material for them to bring into the home or to listen to or see.

One parent came up with an original idea that is hard to refute.

The father listened to all the reasons his children gave for wanting to see a particular PG-13 movie. It had their favorite actors. Everyone else was seeing it. Even church members said it was great. It was rated PG-13 only because of the suggestion of sex—they never really showed it. The language was pretty good—the Lord's name was used in vain only three times in the whole movie.

The teens did admit there was a scene where a building and a bunch of people were blown up, but the violence was just the normal stuff. It wasn't too bad. And, even if there were a few minor things, the special effects were fabulous and the plot was action packed.

However, even with all the justifications the teens made for the PG-13 rating, the father still wouldn't give in. He didn't even give his children a satisfactory explanation for saying no. He just said, "No!"

A little later on that evening, the father asked his teens if they would like some brownies he had baked. He explained that he'd taken the family's favorite recipe and added a little something new. The children asked what it was.

The father calmly replied that he had added dog poop. However, he quickly assured them, *it was only a little bit*. All of the other ingredients were gourmet quality, and he had taken great care to bake the brownies at the precise temperature for the exact time. He was sure the brownies would be superb.

Even with their father's promise that the brownies were of almost perfect quality, the teens would not take any. The father acted surprised. After all, it was only one small part that was causing them to be so stubborn. He was certain they would hardly notice it. Still the teens held firm and would not try the brownies.

The father then told his children how the movie they wanted to see was just like the brownies. Our minds are fooling us into believing that just a little bit of evil won't matter. But the truth is, even a little bit of poop makes the difference between a great treat and something disgusting and totally unacceptable.

The father went on to explain that even though the movie industry would have us believe that most of today's movies are acceptable fare for adults and youth, *they are not*.

Now, when this father's children want to see something that is of questionable material, the father merely asks them if they would like some of his special dog-poop brownies. That closes the subject.

The Ladies Room: Modesty, Mouthiness and Moodiness

The practice of decency and modesty in speech, action and dress is very important for creating an atmosphere suitable for the growth of chastity, but this must be well motivated by respect for one's own body and the dignity of others. Parents, as we have said, should be watchful so that certain immoral fashions and attitudes do not violate the integrity of the home, especially through misuse of the mass media. (TM, no. 56)

Besides the information on modesty in the *Love and Life Student Guide*, many conversations and decisions occurring in the home can enhance your daughter's beauty and virtue by guiding her in choosing modest clothing. It is helpful if the father is strong in his desire to have his daughter dress for respect. He knows what men think when they see teenage girls dressed like half-naked rock stars or women of the street. He can explain to her how men view women who are dressed to entice.

Both parents must realize that their daughter may not understand this at all because she does not have the mind of a man. If her goal of choosing clothing is to fit in with the crowd, she may perceive you—the modesty police—to be her social enemy. Parents, be strong, and wear your title well! As fashions come and go, there seems to be a modern trend toward immodesty. We as consumers must demand more beautiful, not sexy, clothing for our daughters. Parents, please don't give up or give in on the important standards of dress that help your daughter learn how to give and receive respect for herself as a dignified and modest young lady.

As Girls Mature

Growing daughters need thier mother's help in choosing the right bra. Brassieres have to work for the wearer, not just look pretty in the mirror. Their job is to provide support, protection and concealment. In many other countries of the world, these issues are not always as urgent. In the United States, where men have been trained by media ads and television cameramen to look at women's breasts, women need to be extra cautious not to stir up concupiscence. Here, feminine dignity is at stake.

When your daughter begins to develop, even before she needs support, wearing a bra for modesty is important. When you or your daughter purchase a bra, make sure that you get your money's worth. A more modest bra would fit well and be lined, so that it protects and provides a modest covering. The nipples should not be seen through the shirt or blouse, even when the wearer is cold.

As your daughter develops more, or if she is heavy, a bra is important for providing support as well as modesty. A bra should be full enough so that the breasts do not hang out over the bra cup. The bra should also have enough structure so that breasts do not bounce when she is walking. Some daughters need to be reminded that the way they walk could also contribute to this effect.

Your daughter develops quickly during puberty, so check her bra size as often as necessary. Continue to teach her the importance of modesty, protection and support. If your daughter is a dancer or gymnast, or the weather is warm and the outer clothing is lightweight, all three jobs of the bra need to be accomplished with every purchase.

When your daughter is wearing a lightweight blouse or dress, it is always more modest to wear a full covering slip or camisole so that the bra cannot be seen through the shirt. Vests, jackets and sweaters can add more fashion and more modesty to a blouse.

Dressing Up

Shopping for formals is one of the greatest challenges for moms and daughters. Plunging necklines should be avoided or covered, as should deep, sexy slits in the skirts. If the style of the year includes backless or strapless, seek out a style with more coverage if you can. The top of the breast should always be covered. The precaution for backless and strapless dresses is that they are visually enticing for many men. As a compromise, you could use the accompanying stole for fabric and get creative, adding dress straps or a small decorative jacket that can be kept on more easily than a loose stole. Backless dresses still require a bra for modesty, even in a small-breasted girl. If a bra and lining are not built into the dress, purchase a strapless or backless bra as needed to provide modesty, protection and support.

Skirt lengths have been an issue since the fashion trends of the twentieth century. Previously, long flowing clothes provided modesty and feminine beauty. When skirt fashions get short, you can expect a modest length to cover the thigh, even when sitting down. This often means that the skirt should come at least to the top of the knee when standing.

Finally, a modesty check should be done for all clothes that are purchased. Think of all the angles that people will see you from—sitting, standing, looking up at you onstage, looking down at you,

even seeing into a loose armpit or loosely buttoned shirt. For clothes that are so tight you can see your underwear lines, the answer is not skimping on the underwear—it is getting looser clothes!

These modesty arguments are not merely about the amount of fabric on her body. They are about how she is advertising herself—as pure or impure. Modesty is about her reputation as a woman. By her choice of clothing, your daughter will be remembered even in later years when students come home from college, or grow up and look for a husband or wife of their own. Did she dress for respect or dress for attention? To what was she drawing attention? Pray for the strength to persevere in your home campaign for modest dress.

Mouthiness

Teen girls in our era of "women's liberation" have been encouraged to be sassy and insolent. For many years, speaking one's mind without any regard for others, being bossy or mouthing off have become acceptable behavior for young girls. These are not, however, feminine virtues. A young woman growing in virtue can learn to use her wits to control her tongue. Speaking with kindness and respect will help her appear more mature and ladylike.

Meekness is not weakness. Meekness requires the internal strength to be an effective communicator without being obnoxious. Help your daughter grow in meekness and all the virtues. The Blessed Virgin Mary is the ultimate role model for women. She was not aggressive, haughty or gossipy. She was strong, intelligent and prudent. She knew when to speak and when to remain silent. Remind your daughter that she will see many girls become louder and ruder as they physically develop, if they do not know that a girl has to work hard to become virtuous. Encourage her to look to Mary, our Heavenly Mother, for guidance.

Moodiness

Although it was mentioned before, the mother-daughter conversation should continue to include help in managing behavior despite shifting emotions. This is often difficult for young teens, especially when hormones fluctuate daily and they are feeling safe in the comfort of their families. Self-mastery results when we learn to do what is right even when we feel like doing otherwise. It is time for your daughter to practice using her will to overcome impulses, so she does not act according to her whims. Sometimes discipline is necessary if she is not striving for balance herself. A good diet without caffeine, chocolate, sugar and junk food will help reduce the mood shifts. A deeper prayer life will draw her to Christ and His Mother during the confusing times.

> Through a trusting and open dialogue, parents can guide their daughters in facing any emotional perplexity and support the value of Christian chastity out of consideration for the other sex. Instruction for both girls and boys should aim at pointing out the beauty of motherhood and the wonderful reality of procreation as well as the deep meaning of virginity. (TM, no. 92)

Although this course mainly focuses on the goodness of sexuality and virginity, parents can also take this time during adolescence to help their daughter develop skills she may need as a future caretaker, wife, mother and homemaker. Teenage girls can grow in confidence and selflessness as they plan and prepare meals for family and friends, learn creativity through sewing and crafts, learn to care for young children, and study nutrition, health and budgeting.

Men of Honor: Manners, Machismo and Impulsiveness

The Vatican document *The Truth and Meaning of Human Sexuality* again offers advice for mothers and fathers raising sons:

> During puberty the psychological development and emotional development of boys can make them vulnerable to erotic fantasies, and they may

be tempted to try sexual experiences. Parents should be close to their sons and correct the tendency to use sexuality in a hedonistic and materialistic way. Therefore they should remind boys about God's gift, received in order to cooperate with him . . . in this way sons will also learn the respect due to women. (TM, no. 93)

R-e-s-p-e-c-t

By your word and example, it is important to teach your sons to treat girls and women with respect and courtesy. Manners from childhood should be improved, not forgotten, when they notice the girls become women. Young men need to practice treating women with respect in order to really prove their manhood. Basic courtesies of opening doors, avoiding gross vulgarity and denigrating humor, and speaking respectful language show respect for the dignity of women.

"Macho Man" is a phrase describing men who misuse their power or strength to oppress or demean women. A boy or young man may think it necessary to "prove" his misunderstood masculinity, and that the way to do this is through early dating, controlling women or pursuing sexual conquests. Help your sons resist this temptation, which is prevalent in some peer groups. Make it clear that the young man who proves real masculine strength is the one who respects women and controls his thoughts, desires and actions.

Who rules? Christ rules! Introduce your son to a deeper relationship with Christ, whose strength he will need during the teen years. Christ is a real man's model of love, kindness, humility, courage and strength. He went to His death for our sakes. Macho men are really insecure, not strong. They use control or put down women in order to feel better about themselves. A macho man is not truly masculine; he is weak. A man of character is one who has self-control and who is capable of sacrificing himself for others.

Custody of the Senses and Avoiding Pornography

In modern American society we are surrounded by revealing images of beautiful women. While it is not necessary for men to wear blindfolds all the time, they must train their eyes to look away and train their minds to resist temptations. A quick flick of the remote control against immodest commercials and shows is just the beginning. Remind them to seek God in prayer to control their curiosities and stay physically involved in sports and activities.

Pornography is everywhere. It invites itself into our lives. Teach your sons to consider it as a poison to their soul and to their ability to really love. Work with them to see young women they meet as beautiful children of God, not objects for men's enjoyment.

> Chastity includes an *apprenticeship in self-mastery* which is training in human freedom. The alternative is clear: either man governs his passions and finds peace, or he lets himself be dominated by them and becomes unhappy.
> —*Catechism of the Catholic Church,* no. 2339

Have your sons be quick to turn their eyes away from young women who are dressed immodestly, and they will gain, for Christ, "custody of the eyes".

Emotional maturity is the ability to think before we act. Teenage boys have a tendency to be impulsive rather than thoughtful, but they can conquer these tendencies. Angry feelings do not have to lead to violence; passionate feelings do not have to lead to lust; jealousy and hatred do not have to lead to revenge. Remind your son that he does not need to act according to his feelings, but can channel his impulses into other constructive outlets. A real man practices self-control.

To help your son conquer his impulsiveness and develop his character, show him how to apply the virtues of diligence, patience, honesty, kindness and self-control to his studies, sports, skills and home life. Help him work each day to become a man of internal strength. Teach him to develop his will power by participating in activities that are challenging. Encourage him to seek out hard work, tough sports and giant mountains to climb. Show him how to see bad weather as a chance to get tough, not to stay inside; challenge him to perform more difficult tasks for the household. Teach him to strengthen his body with activities and his soul with his daily prayer life.

Adolescence is also a great time for dads to help their sons develop skills that will help them later in life with financial responsibility, home repairs, building and carpentry, electronics, car maintenance, investments and other life skills. This is not only a good use of time now that saves him money later, but it helps a young man grow in confidence as he acquires these new skills and responsibilities. Your son's preparation for manhood includes caring for himself and for a possible family in the future.

Two-Minute Mastery for Busy Dads

Men and Self-Mastery
Teach your sons that men can gain self-mastery by a) training the will b) growing in prayer and, c) fasting

A. Training the will:
   1. Do things you don't want to do until it is no longer unpleasant. Then your will has become stronger.
   2. Deprive yourself of something pleasant like a dessert, snack, favorite television program, golf outing, etc. without complaining or grumbling
   3. Set definite goals and quotas for yourself like the amount of jobs you do, minutes of exercise, number of pushups and sit-ups. Do this consistently until the will is trained to accept this as normal.
   4. Do something that you think is difficult like extra reading or studying, getting out of bed half an hour early, or taking a difficult hike.

B. Growing in prayer
   1. Know that mastery of the will over the flesh cannot be achieved on our own without God's grace, but God wants to help you.
   2. Keep a regular program of daily prayer, with particular times of union with God morning, noon and night.
   3. Spend ten minutes a day in silence with God.
   4. Frequent the sacraments of Penance and Eucharist.

C. Fasting
   1. Jesus Christ began his years of ministry by fasting.
   2. Fasting is the most effective means of gaining self-mastery.
   3. Fasting is a type of prayer, in which we humble ourselves before God, deny ourselves of some material thing we have a right to have, and sincerely seek the assistance of God.

Real Men Practice Chastity

How will chastity help your son become more masculine? Only by following the will of God can a man become the best person God made him to be.

A. A chaste man avoids harm to his body and soul that hinders his ability to accept adult responsibility.
   1. Obeying God brings him freedom and happiness. Sexual sin brings him misery.

   2. Sexual sin distracts him from his work and worthy goals in life.
   3. Sin causes natural guilt, which leads to confusion, mental distress, and escapist behaviors.
   4. A man who regularly gives in to sexual temptation loses the grace he needs to make wise decisions and hear God's answers to his prayers. Without grace, a man is left only to his own efforts in his family life and work.

B. A young man who practices chastity can more easily attain the happiness God intends for him.
   1. He has more strength to resist temptations.
   2. He has the peace of mind that comes with moral maturity.
   3. He can more easily practice Natural Family Planning in marriage.
   4. He can teach chastity to his own children with greater conviction.
   5. Self-control brings greater strength and health to the individual man, which can prolong sexual function and satisfaction in marriage.
   6. Purity is the greatest gift he can give to his future wife and the surest foundation for a fulfilling marriage.
   7. A chaste man has already learned to love well where the majority of love in marriage takes place, outside of the bedroom.
   8. A chaste man is more trustworthy and admirable. He will be respected by his wife even more because she can more easily feel safe and secure with him.

Is Your Teen Ready to Date?

Because good relationships are important in life, it is unfair to leave your child to find his own way in the current dating scene of hormones, emotions and using one another for temporary pleasure. Too often

the young—with fluctuating emotions and limited social skills—are left to follow their feelings, seal them with a kiss and continue through life, with a series of broken hearts or regrets, on an emotional roller coaster.

Review the chapters in the *Student Guide* on emotional maturity, modesty and dating. Then discuss together some standards for relationships before your teen even begins flirting, handholding or kissing. Discuss your child's goals in life and the positive use of social time in light of his personal growth. Help him become aware that dating can help or hinder his maturity during the teen years, depending on how it is approached.

Before dating begins, a teen should be able to:

- Identify the purpose of dating, which is to find a marriage partner.

- Have self-knowledge, knowing one's values, talents, temperament, character strengths and weaknesses. How else can a person recognize who may be a good marriage partner?
- Have direction and focus in life; knowing what type of person one wants to be as an adult, and what steps need to be taken to become that person.
- Have years of practice in courtesy, manners and consideration of others. Otherwise a teen would attract others who do not treat people well, either.
- Practice patience and kindness at home and with friends, knowing that this is how real love begins. Otherwise one's poor date may become a victim of his criticism and manipulation.
- Understand that learning to love is practicing unselfishness, often to the point of sacrifice, for the good of the other person. Otherwise the relationships would be rooted in pleasure seeking.
- Have extensive practice in self-discipline so that sexual self-discipline is not a foreign concept.
- Be capable of carrying on social conversations for an entire evening with people of both sexes and different age groups, or else real personal growth cannot take place during the date.
- If your teen is a young man, he should have the financial means to pay for dates and the ability to provide transportation.

Without ensuring these criteria are met, it would be unfair of you to let your teens date. You would be setting them up to fail in their dating years and in their future marriage. A good practice to develop in the dating preparation years (normally ages fourteen to seventeen) is to plan supervised co-ed activities where friendships can be developed without the pressures of pairing off. Teens need to have had many good friends of both sexes before they can even assess who they are and what type of people they should date.

The Road to Social Failure

Teens who don't know themselves, their talents, character strengths or weaknesses

Can lose self in romance and feelings, find identity only in boy or girlfriend.

Feel lost, unloved if they don't have a regular date. Socially dependent.

Settle for whomever gives them attention at the time.

Teens who have no direction or focus in life

Will become like their peers in order to fit in or belong.

Will fail to grow in conviction and the inner strength that comes from it.

Will suffer from low self-esteem, low achievement.

Teens who demonstrate little or no manners or consideration

Think they are "being themselves", when they are really being lazy or thoughtless.

Attract only those with low standards.

Find no reason to achieve growth in character.

Teens who are unkind, impatient

Thrive on criticism, sarcasm and put-downs; frequently argue.

Often enter into manipulative and controlling relationships of possession rather than love and freedom.

Their social life becomes an emotional drain, leaving a negative view of life, love and relationships.

Teens who are self-centered

Use people to fill selfish desires for popularity, security, or the emotional high of feeling good.

See others as objects to be used for one's own gratification.

Are unable to be generous in other areas of life; are often intolerant of others who do not please them at all times.

Teens who are undisciplined, or lack self-discipline

Find it difficult to be responsible for time and energy. Are more likely to act on feelings or hormones.

Cannot control affections or behaviors; are often morally challenged.

Fall easily into self-destruction or immoral behaviors.

Teens who lack communication or conversation skills, or are extremely shy

Avoid or fear quiet time with groups or on dates. May use alcohol to escape insecurity. Often use movies, television and music to escape chances for conversation.

Often move from videos to kissing with little time spent getting to know each other as persons.

Their relationships have no basis in common interests or ideals. With only time and feelings in common, relationships are rootless.

(Originally published in a slightly different form in *Sex Respect: The Option of True Sexual Freedom, The Parent Guide.* Coleen Kelly Mast. Copyright 2001. Respect Incorporated, P.O. Box 349, Bradley, IL. p. 56.)

Giving Directions for Dating

It is important to be specific. Adolescents are in the toddler stage of their sexuality. Just like a two-year-old crossing the street, they need specific directions because they cannot see the whole picture yet. They need to be told that passionate affection and sexual intercourse belong only in marriage. They need to know it is unfair and wrong to try to arouse the passions of another person when those passions can in no way be satisfied outside the commitment of marriage. Adolescents need to know that if they find themselves becoming too "worked up", they should stop the activity, go to a place where they are not alone and tempted, or end the date.

Here are three good rules of thumb:

1. Keep all of your clothes all the way on all of the time.
2. Don't let any part of anyone else's body get anywhere between you and your clothes.
3. Avoid arousal.

Teens need to know that using alcohol and drugs is wrong and especially dangerous when dating because their freedom to make good moral decisions is compromised. The mind gets clouded up and is unable to make good judgements.

We need to teach teens how to say *no*—not "probably not" or "I don't think so", but *no*.

We can teach them to say no to any pressure to do wrong, and they can do so assertively and kindly without putting the other person down or becoming defensive.

Positive Talk about Dating

If you expect your son to date, you should educate him in the ways of respectful dating. With boys it's an excellent idea to discuss these points:

- How to be courteous and respectful
- How girls' emotions differ from boys'
- How to carry on a conversation that shows interest in the girl as a person
- How to dance without hanging on each other

- How to practice self-control in all areas of his life, including his sexual drives
- How to say good-night without being passionate
- How he can be the leader on the date by planning time and activities well
- How he will assume any financial expenses of the date

With girls, parents find the following points of discussion helpful:

- How she can set the tone of the relationship by the way she acts
- How modesty is important in helping boys respect her
- How she receives from others the same respect she has for herself
- How boys can be aroused much more easily, sometimes even with just an embrace
- How to carry on a conversation that shows genuine interest in her date
- What responsibility she has in setting limits, and how a well-mannered boy will be grateful
- What boys are thinking (best done by you, Dad!)

These conversations should not be just mother to daughter and father to son. It would be helpful to have the perspective of both parents in these areas.

Setting Limits

We can eliminate some of the pressures on our teens by setting limits for them.

> If my parents let me stay out 'til 2 or 3 in the morning, I would think it was great at first . . . then I would begin to wonder if they really loved me. (a sixteen-year-old girl)

Setting limits and requirements for daily routines such as meals, homework, television, curfews, extracurricular activities and household chores enhances basic household order and personal development. Setting limits on dating and social outings can assist in the development of chastity and eliminate the possibilities of other pressures.

Here are some suggestions:

1. Give your teen a chance to prove he or she is responsible by setting curfews for all social outings. Allowing them to stay out late is asking for trouble.
2. Setting an age for dating can relieve the pressure a teen may feel to begin dating. However, be careful to set it high enough so that you do not contribute to the pressure of finding a date before he's ready. Many families choose the age of sixteen. This gives teens a chance to get settled in high school, develop some wholesome relationships and avoid those who are "on the prowl". It also gives them a chance to display some responsibility before being given this privilege. Most of all, setting a dating age gives teens something to look forward to and slows down the rush to grow up.
3. Establish dating rules clearly. Deciding on a reasonable curfew is not only responsible, but it gives your teen a sense of security. Always provide teens with a good excuse to go home at a decent hour. Most really don't want to stay out half the night, but few have the maturity yet to set their own limits.

- Discuss the dangers and forbid dates alone at someone's house. Talk about the temptations privacy affords.
- Discuss the types of public places to go and the kinds of movies to see on dates.
- Encourage group dating and double dating, and forbid the steady dating of one particular person, until they are out of high school. Protect your teens from the pressures of serious relationships when they are too young to marry.

4. Guide teens to set limits on affection, so that affection does not become passion. If such limits are decided with a clear head before dating, they won't have to be negotiated later.
5. Help your teens learn to control their emotions by talking to them frequently about their relationships and offering them your perspective. Highly emotional relationships drain energy that should be used in school, church and family activities.
6. Teach teens to balance their lives. Encourage them to become involved in constructive activities. This helps set limits on their own tendencies to focus on the emotional turmoil of adolescence. The old adage remains true; idleness is the devil's workshop.

Keep Trying, Parents: You're Not Alone

There are many parents all over the world working with their teens to develop character and virtue. Most parents, believing that their children are good, want to do what is right. These parents believe in God's plan and are striving to live it in their families, too.

By getting together with other concerned parents in your church and community, you can reinforce each other's efforts. It is important to meet the parents of your children's friends and discuss your values and expectations with them. We can find moral support in our church and parent-teacher organizations.

Finally, remember that God is always with us.

When Teens Fail

Even if we honestly do everything within our power to promote chastity in our homes, we still don't have total control over our teen's decisions. Our children have a free will and have human weaknesses like everyone else. With a weak moment, a failure in chastity can occur.

Some telltale signs of a sexually active youth include

- Spending more time *alone* with one person
- Evidence of passionate encounters when coming home, like clothes in disarray
- Not talking much, especially about dates
- Showing less interest in other friends

A sure way to find out is simply to ask. Whether a teen will admit it or not, if there are sufficient grounds for suspicion, it would be appropriate to remind a teen of what is expected and the consequences of failure to practice self-control.

Passion is the worst preparation for marriage. Unmarried people should not try to arouse sexual passion. Clothing should never be opened or removed to provide body parts as playthings. People are not toys. This is a poor attitude to bring into a marriage.

Even if a teen has gone too far, it is still possible to turn back, repent and stay pure. Parents should

offer support in this conversion effort, even if it requires helping their teen discontinue a relationship. Point out again the natural consequences, like sexually transmitted diseases, emotional pain and pregnancy. Say that you expect the relationship to stop and that you will be willing to talk to the other person about it if necessary. Take them to confession for the mercy and spiritual relief that only God can provide. Take them to the doctor for a blood test and treatment for hidden sexually transmitted diseases (STDs) if necessary. Love your teen enough to help him change.

Human beings are made to give and receive love. We were made to give of ourselves and to discover and fulfill ourselves in the process. To reduce human relationships to sexual encounters is demeaning. Using women or manipulating men is not joyful or fulfilling. Although it might be temporarily gratifying, it is not uplifting or nourishing to either the man or the woman.

The immaturity of physically based relationships can stunt a person's ability to love. Young people get trapped in these empty relationships because they don't understand sex. They are not free. They have temporarily lost their ability to love. A nineteen-year-old young man wisely admitted the truth about his sexual relationship: "I wasn't sure my love was for real because I enjoyed the sex so much. . . . But how will I ever know this is love if I continue the sex?" The truth is, he won't, without a change in behavior.

Time for Conversion

Renewing one's virginity invites teens to a new understanding of love. First, the love of God can be increased through an experience of His mercy in the Sacrament of Reconciliation. Secondly, love can be seen in a different light when one has already seen the sin of fornication for what it is. Stopping the habit of physical pleasure without real intimacy can awaken in your teen a new awareness of the real need to love and be loved. Challenging teens to raise their standards of love will help them attract others with high standards. Continuing the pattern of sexual promiscuity will lead only to unhappiness. Sexuality needs to be raised to the highest standard

because it is connected so deeply to the meaning of life and love. Invite those who have misunderstood love and sex to stop their current sexual patterns long enough to open their eyes to the reality of love as it could be. Encourage your teens to find ways to develop their talents and give of themselves in a way that will enable them to develop good habits of unselfishness and sharing with others. Experiencing the fulfillment that comes with generous love will help them outgrow their former habits of using others or being used sexually. Their capacity to love can grow.

Parents of teens who are renewing their virginity should be extra helpful in encouraging new patterns of behavior. Beware: Stopping sexual activity will not automatically solve all of your teen's problems. Instead, it may reawaken the emptiness or insecurity they were trying to cover up with sexual pleasure. Other concerns may also need to be addressed. A young person involved in sex outside of marriage is looking for love in the wrong places. As a parent, love him, and try to guide him toward paths of real love and giving of himself that provide true fulfillment. For the parent of a sexually experienced teen, this is an important time to forge a better relationship with your teen. First of all, include forgiveness instead of condemnation, sympathy instead of righteousness, understanding instead of coldness. And never give up on praying for your teen's conversion. God can do anything!

For additional practical tips, there is an entire chapter dedicated to the concept of secondary virginity in the book *Sex Respect: The Option of True Sexual Freedom* written by this author and published by Respect Incorporated.

Birth Control for Teens: Why Not?

Birth control for teens is a big mistake.

A survey of high school students asked those who were virgins why they chose to remain that way. Here are the most popular answers:

1. Fear of getting pregnant
2. Not wanting to disappoint parents

A parent who gives a teen birth control information and materials has destroyed both reasons. By encouraging sexual activity, they are in effect saying, "Do it, but don't get caught". If teens were told there would be no security systems or personnel in the shopping center next weekend, might there be an increase in shoplifting?

Giving teens birth control materials so they can continue to fornicate is like putting a bandage on cancer. The problem of immature and immoral sexuality is deep and growing and internal. Teen pregnancy is only a sign of disordered sexual activity. Pregnancy is not a disease. Birth control addresses only the outward appearances. Besides, the only 100 percent effective birth control is abstinence.

Even teens themselves have seen that abstinence is better than birth control. A group of teenagers, unwed but involved in a pregnancy, were asked these questions:

1. What do you say to a teen who is sexually active?

   The teens responded:

- Confront them.
- Ask them why.
- Tell them, "If that's your definition of love, you're wrong."

- Keep after them so they will avoid the problems we had to face.
- Cut down on free time alone; otherwise, the temptation is too hard to resist.

2. How do you keep after a teen without being nosy?

   The teens answered:

- If you didn't care, you wouldn't ask.
- Kids are irrational anyway; take the risk.
- Tell them that they must follow your rules as long as they live in your house. Then write down the rules so they're clear.

3. What if the teen doesn't seem to care and brazenly breaks house rules?
   The experienced teens responded: It's probably a cover-up. Rebellious teens are crying out for help, and they don't even know it.

An interesting thought for girls was written by Donna Steichen in the pamphlet "How to Be Your Own Woman" (Human Life Center). It responds to the question, "What if you are in love . . . if your emotions as well as your body urge you to go ahead?"

Isn't it free and independent, then, to do what you both want?

Stop for a moment. See what you have agreed to.

You want to please him because you love him. He says he loves you—and he wants you to please him.

Are you in love with each other?

Or are both of you in love with him?

Love makes people unselfish. When you love someone, you want to do what's best for that person—to protect and cherish your beloved.

If he loves you, he will want what's best for you. Sex before marriage is not best for you. It isn't best for him, either.

Unwed Parents

If a daughter becomes pregnant, or a son fathers a child out of wedlock, remember the baby is not a "mistake"; it is a human life. A girl who has been severely threatened not to become pregnant will be under tremendous pressure to destroy the evidence by killing the baby. Although having an unwed, pregnant daughter is always a disappointment for a parent, we must pull ourselves together and think of the daughter and her baby and not of our own embarrassment.

Pregnancy is not a sin; fornication is. The unwed pregnancy is a result of wrong sexual activity; however, a further and even more serious wrong is to punish the innocent baby with a cruel death by abortion.

As Jesus would do, we must forgive and then go on to make moral choices considering all involved, including the baby.

In the event of an untimely pregnancy, please seek counsel at a pro-life organization like Birthright or Catholic Charities. Individuals at these organizations are trained to help you and your daughter deal with the emotions and decisions involved.

Marriage

Teens deciding to marry based on pregnancy have the odds against them. A small percentage (15–20 percent) of these marriages do work, by the grace of God, if all other reasons to marry are positive. In most cases of teen pregnancy, however, marriage is not the best solution, mostly because the immaturity that led to pregnancy is not a good foundation for marriage.

Raising the Child

So who raises the child? The young unwed mother alone? Parenting goes beyond holding cute little babies. Children need parental protection and guidance for many years. Mothers and fathers are responsible for providing not only physical care, but also good example, moral direction, loving correction and clear discipline. These should all be considered when making decisions regarding who will raise the child. If the young woman wants to keep the baby,

· ·

explain that she will need help. Consider the implications—good and bad—of grandparents helping raise the child. Many grandparents have taken on that task, but it does require a certain amount of heroism and sacrifice.

Adoption

The benefits of adoption are threefold: The unwed mother can continue to work toward future goals, becoming more prepared to be a wife and mother at a future date. The baby can enjoy the love, care and protection possible in a two-parent home. The adopting parents can add to their family with a baby to love, enjoy and care for. The pain and sacrifice of giving the child to a loving couple may be worth the better opportunity the child will have for a happier life.

The Pledge for Purity

Chapter 24 of the *Love and Life* student workbook includes a pledge for purity. It is written in a box, but it is also available in the form of pledge cards that are available at www.loveandlife.com. At a certain birthday, after completing this course together or before beginning to date, invite your teen to take the pledge for chastity.

The Challenge to Be Pure in Thoughts, Words and Actions

In order to honor God, respect myself and affirm the dignity of love and life:

> *I promise to practice chastity from now on, and in the future vocation to which God calls me.*

Signature_____ Date_____

Upon completion of the *Love and Life* program,

witnessed by_____
(parent or teacher)

Wallet-sized copies of this pledge card are available at www.loveandlife.com

PARISH IMPLEMENTATION OF LOVE AND LIFE

Assistance for Parents

Church directives on education in human sexuality have always been clear regarding the primary role of the parents. The role of pastors and instructors delegated by them is to provide the authentic moral teaching of the Catholic Church to those parents who require assistance.

There are various ways of helping and supporting parents in fulfilling their fundamental right and duty to educate their children for love. Such assistance never means taking from parents or diminishing their formative right and duty, because they remain "original and primary", "irreplaceable and inalienable". Therefore, the role which others can carry out in helping parents is always (a) subsidiary, because the formative role of the family is always preferable, and (b) subordinate, that is, subject to the parents' attentive guidance and control. Everyone must observe the right order of cooperation and collaboration between parents and those who can help them in their task. It is clear that the assistance of others must be given first and foremost to parents rather than to their children.

Those who are called to help parents in educating their children for love must be disposed and prepared to teach in conformity with the authentic moral doctrine of the Catholic Church. Moreover, they must be mature persons, of a good moral reputation, faithful to their own Christian state of life, married or single, laity, religious or priests. They must not only be prepared in the details of moral and sexual information but they must also be sensitive to the rights and role of parents and the family, as well as the needs and problems of children and young people. In this way, in the light of the principles and content of this guide, they must enter "into the same spirit that animates parents". But if parents believe themselves to be capable of providing an adequate education for love, they are not bound to accept assistance. (TM, nos. 145 and 146)

Teaching Methods

The Pontifical Council for the Family recommends these five methods for providing parents with the assistance they need to teach their children sexual morality. The normal and fundamental method of teaching sexual morality is *personal dialogue between parents and their children*. There is no substitute for this dialogue, for it is parents who most love and respect their children as individuals and understand their various stages of development. When parents seek help from the Church, the Vatican advises the following methods:

1. As couples or as individuals, parents can *meet with others who are prepared for education for love* to draw on their experience and competence. These people can offer explanations and provide parents with books and other resources approved by the ecclesiastical authorities.

2. Parents who are not always prepared to face up to the problematic side of education for love can take part in meetings with their children, guided by expert persons who are worthy of trust, for example, doctors, priests or educators. In some cases, in the interest of greater freedom of expression, meetings in which only daughters or sons are present are preferable.

3. In certain situations, parents can *entrust part of education for love to another trustworthy person,* if

there are matters which require a specific competence or pastoral care in particular cases.

4. *Catechesis on morality* may be provided by other trustworthy persons, with particular emphasis on sexual ethics at puberty and adolescence. Parents should take an interest in the moral catechesis which is given to their own children outside the home and use it as a support for their own educational work. Such catechesis must not include the more intimate aspects of sexual information, whether biological or affective, which belong to individual formation within the family.

5. The *religious formation of the parents themselves,* in particular solid catechetical preparation of adults in the truth of love, builds the foundations of a mature faith that can guide them in the formation of their own children. This adult catechesis enables them not only to deepen their understanding of the community of life and love in marriage, but also helps them learn how to communicate better with their own children. Furthermore, in the very process of forming their children in love, parents will find that they benefit much, because they will discover that this ministry of love helps them to "maintain a living awareness of the 'gift' they continually receive from their children". To make parents capable of carrying out their educational work, special formation courses with the help of experts can be promoted. (TM, nos. 130–34)

The *Love and Life* student and parent guides are designed to meet all of these recommendations of the Vatican.

1. First and foremost, the parish can introduce the *Love and Life* program to parents of adolescents at a parent meeting. For support and accountability, it would be good for the parents to meet once a month for four months to discuss each of the four units and how the teaching is going at home. In adherence with the Church recommendations, take care to see that the group discussion leaders are in adherence to Church teachings. Parish workers should be careful to realize that many parents these days did not learn and do not live the Church's teachings on sexuality. No matter how well they lead other events in the parish, they must not be given a teaching role if they are not properly formed.

2. Father/son and mother/daughter programs are the second recommendation from the Pontifical Council. The revised *Love and Life* program has moved all of the intimate aspects of sexual information into the *Parent Guide,* so it is appropriate for use at father/son or mother/daughter group presentations. The parent can be assigned certain chapters to cover at home after or between sessions. Parish leaders for these sessions can receive training for this type of presentation by contacting www.loveandlife.com or www.sexrespect.com, or by inviting the author of this text to provide training through the diocese.

3. The third recommendation by the Pontifical Council is for parents whose teens need specific counseling for problems such as masturbation, sexual abuse, pornography addictions, or for parents who are struggling themselves with living God's teachings. The parish may have competent professionals for referrals, priests who can provide spiritual direction, or NFP teachers who are capable of teaching sexual morality in a private setting.

4. The fourth recommendation is that catechesis in morality be provided through the parish or school. This normally includes the study of the Ten Commandments, as well as corresponding teachings from the *Catechism of the Catholic Church*. Chapters from the *Love and Life: Student Guide* can be used for this catechesis in religion classes on the following topics: the Fall

of Man (Chapters 3 and 4), the Sacraments as a source of grace (Chapter 5), developing virtues and good friendships (Chapters 6, 7 and 8), overcoming temptations (Chapters 12 and 13) and the saints as role models (Chapter 18). Parents should oversee the catechesis to make sure it is in line with the Church, delicately presented at the appropriate ages, and does not include the biological or affective intimate aspects, which belong to individual formation within the family.

5. The fifth recommendation is education for the parents themselves. There is no substitute for adult education. Jesus taught the adults and played with the children, and our parishes often teach the children and only play with the adults. Small study groups of parents can read and discuss together any of the Church teachings recommended in the following section of this book. Other sound adult formation programs are available to help us learn to love God and our families better.

In the face of many challenges to Christian chastity, the gifts of nature and grace, which parents enjoy, always remain the most solid foundations on which the church forms her children. Much of the formation in the home is indirect, incarnated in a loving and tender atmosphere, for it arises from the presence and example of parents whose love is pure and generous. If parents are given confidence in this talk of education for love, they will be inspired to overcome the challenges and problems of our times by their own ministry of love.

In this noble task, may parents always place their trust in God through prayer to the Holy Spirit. (TM, nos. 149, 150)

SUGGESTIONS FOR FURTHER READING

1. *The Truth and Meaning of Human Sexuality,* Pontifical Council for the Family. 1995. Provides guidelines and objectives, as well as ages and stages for human sexuality education. It gives parents the information and confidence to do their job well.

2. *Educational Guidance in Human Love,* Congregation for Catholic Education, 1983. This is an outline for sex education in the home and provides guidelines for educators as well.

3. *Familiaris Consortio: (The Role of the Christian Family in the Modern World),* Pope John Paul II. 1981.
   The beautiful teaching on the family in the modern world by Pope John Paul II. Gain hope and specific suggestions for the families in today's world as they are challenged to live as Christian witnesses.

4. *The Vatican Declaration on Sexual Ethics,* Sacred Congregation for the Doctrine of the Faith. 1974.
   Teachings based on divine and natural law regarding premarital sex and masturbation, cohabitation, homosexuality and other issues. Includes discussion of occasions of sin and pastoral applications.

5. *Humanae Vitae,* Pope Paul VI. 1968.
   Describes the beauty and dignity of men and women in their role as married couples and co-creators of life. Includes some of the most beautiful and prophetic writings on love, marriage and human dignity that ever have been published.

6. *Evangelium Vitae (The Gospel of Life),* Pope John Paul II. 1995.
   Speaks of the dignity of the human person, and offers an understanding of the morality behind pro-life issues.

7. *Donum Vitae (The Gift of Life),* Congregation for the Doctrine of the Faith. 1987.
   The Vatican document that helps us understand technological reproduction, sterility treatments and laboratory conception.

8. *The Catechism of the Catholic Church.* 1997. Written in four sections: Our Beliefs, The Sacraments, The Moral Life and Prayer. Clarifies and summarizes the teachings of the Catholic Church.

All of these documents are available online.

Additional Resources

1. www.loveandlife.com A website for chastity materials to supplement this *Love and Life* series.

2. www.sexrespect.com A website devoted to *Sex Respect: The Option of True Sexual Freedom,* the world's leading abstinence program, also written by Coleen Kelly Mast.

3. www.catholic.com Chastity information by Jason Evert.

4. www.reallove.net Chastity resources by Mary Beth Bonocci.

5. www.ccli.org The Couple to Couple League, a marriage-support organization that promotes Natural Family Planning.

6. www.couragerc.net The website for Courage, a Catholic support group for men and women suffering from homosexual inclinations.

7. www.popepaulvi.com The Pope Paul VI Institute offers help for infertile couples and those interested in Natural Family Planning.